Southern-Fried
and Horrified

Ronald Kelly

STYGIAN
S K Y
M E D I A

Southern Fried and Horrified

Copyright © 2022 by Ronald Kelly

Published by Stygian Sky Media, LLC

30011 Commons Royal View Dr.

Huffman, TX 77336

ISBN 978-1-63951-082-5 (paperback)

ISBN 978-1-63951-100-6 (hardcover)

ISBN 978-1-63951-099-3 (ebook)

First U.S. Edition November 2022

Contents

This book is dedicated to those who loved and supported me and my writing career throughout the years, as well as those who influenced me creatively in my formative years, but who are no longer among us.

Earline and Robert Kelly
Clara and John Alexander Spicer
Ora and Alfred Kelley
Carrol Clemons
Jack Hunter Daves
Ray Bradbury
Robert Bloch
Richard Matheson
Manly Wade Wellman
Forrest J. Ackerman
Charles Grant
Karl Edward Wagner
David B. Silva
J.F. Gonzalez
Mark Justice
Butch Hewitt
Frank Michaels Errington
Jon Recluse

Introduction

Writers are all about stories.

Reading them, creating them, writing them, selling and publishing them. And then there's living them. Usually, that's the one that folks never know or hear about. If it's written down at all, it's usually in journals or diaries; private thoughts and secret angsts they've wrestled with and endured, behind the keyboard or elsewhere. Most of the time it's things that's best forgotten or not to be dwelled on; lost opportunities, anthology deadlines missed, rejections... pages upon pages of them.

Or maybe it has nothing to do with writing at all. Maybe the story involves their life in general. Mundanely dull or stressful to the point of overload and devastation. A difficult, abusive upbringing or happy idyllic childhood. Where they lived or when. The kinds of movies they watched and books they read. Whether they were bullied as a child... or, perhaps, were the bully themselves.

That kind of thing is what forges a writer and gives them the drive to do it, day after day. To take little bits and pieces of things in their head, like useless scrap from a junkyard, and build entire worlds. To deem themselves the God of Prose and conjure living, breathing characters that you love or hate, loathe or feel pity for. Some writers have a knack for pushing all the buttons in all the right ways; making you so angry you could strangle someone who is only made of words on a page or causing you to weep bitterly for a person who is merely a figment of the author's imagination, brought to life in broad strokes of creativity and raw emotion.

Sometimes, a writer feels the need to shelf their fictional worlds for a short while and reflect on the real one... the one they grew up in, smiled and agonized

through, loved and grieved in. Some believe their journey thus far to be utterly uninteresting and lackluster... sort of like searching for their reflection in the murky surface of a mud puddle. Others, fueled by ego and arrogance, believe that their story will put all others to same, when, in fact, all they are doing is bragging and lifting annoyance and resentment to fresh new levels. Every now and then, if an author is famous enough, popular enough, or respected enough, they feel compelled to share their story... and others desire to hear it in return.

I may not fit into any of the categories mentioned above, but I do have a story to tell. One that started over sixty years ago and includes a writing career that has spanned thirty-six years to date. Most folks who know Ol' Ron – both recently or since the dinosaur days – know me as a straight-shooting, honest type of fella, willing to tell you how it is now or was back then, without pandering, pulling punches, or kissing ass. If I tell you a story, it's going to be one forged from the heart and soul, sincere and straight to the point. Sometimes I can make you smile like a briar-chewing mule, while other times I can make you break down and cry... ugly sobbing with snot-slinging and all. That's just the way I am. Always have been and always will.

When I took to social media and made my desire known to pen a memoir of sorts, sprinkled liberally with writing advice and anecdotes, the response was positively unanimous. When Brian Keene, one of the finest horror authors of his generation and well into the next, tweets "Please, please, please, please!" in response, then you know, if Brian wants it, well, hell... you've just got to go and do it.

The Ronald Kelly you will read about during the course of this book may or may not be the one you are familiar with. There have been many evolutions and incarnations over the years; the introverted but imaginative child, the awkward, painfully shy nerd, the angry young man with lofty aspirations that constantly alluded him. Then, later, the small press author who scored a cherished place in mass market publishing and lost it almost as quickly, the bitter and disillusioned has-been who walked away for a decade, and the one who rediscovered his first love, took a deep breath, and gathered the nerve to give it all one more try.

So, sit on down there and let me tell you story... one that I know by heart. And, on the way, we'll talk about books and movies and influences and the business of laying our souls bare on the printed page. I promise to keep it as truthful and engaging as I can manage... whether it tickles like a feather or cuts deeply like the edge of a razor.

As Jerry and the Dead used to sing... what a long, strange trip it's been.

And it has been... so far.

Ronald Kelly
Brush Creek, Tennessee
January 2022

Accolades

"Pull up a comfy chair—Ronald Kelly has a story to tell! An absolutely fascinating memoir with a generous helping of writing advice sprinkled in, this book is a must-read not only for his rabid fans, but anybody with an interest in the horror genre. It's laugh-out-loud funny, heartbreaking, infuriating, and inspiring—this book is as good as it gets."
— Jeff Strand, author of *Dweller*

"Southern-Fried and Horrified is going to stick with me for the rest of my life. It covers everything an ardent Horror fiend could want: social and racial commentary, the history of Horror from the 80s to present day, interspersed with helpful grits and bits on the writing trade. I've heard some of the stories in here from Ron before, yet, they landed a gut punch and choked me up as if it were my first time hearing them. Some even made me bust out laughing! From time-to-time Ron displays that any challenge that comes his way, he's going to beat it. His unquenchable thirst to craft a story and share with the rest of us is not only inspiring, but it's reflective of the human species as a whole--always in need of a story, even if it's one you heard a time or two. Ronald Kelly is a name that not only deserves, but *demands* a legacy that matches the likes of Mark Twain, L. Frank Baum, and

Richard Matheson. If you love Horror, you'll love and learn real quick why you need this memoir in your life."
-- Patrick R. McDonough, Producer/host of Dead Headspace podcast

"The origin story of a true hero of the horror genre. Ronald Kelly unearths his past, bares his soul, and shows his love of a craft that is never easy, rarely forgiving, yet so rewarding. This will sit on my shelf right next to King's *On Writing*. A treasure to be rediscovered over and over."
-- Hunter Shea, author of *Creature* and *To the Devil, A Cryptid*

"Ronald Kelly's *Southern-Fried & Horrified* isn't just the story of how Ol' Ron's tales came to fruition. It's the story of how the man came to be, and shaped these worlds and characters that make you laugh, make you cry, and because this is horror, scare the pants off you. Combined with a lifetime's worth of writing tips and some fun facts, this memoir does what the best stories are supposed to do. Makes you feel every word and learn a little something along the way."
-- Brennan LaFaro, author of *Slattery Falls*

"Ronald Kelly writes about the joys and pitfalls of the writing life with wisdom, warmth, and wit. An inspirational and entertaining memoir from a veteran horror scribe who's survived – and thrived – in the all-too-often heartbreaking world of publishing. A must-read for both writers and fans!"
– Tim Waggoner, author of *Writing in the Dark*

Chapter One

In the Beginning

(and even a little bit before)

M y parents came from hard-working, rural stock. Hardscrabble tobacco farmers and those who worked in greasy factories or drove big machinery that unsettled the dust of the earth, furrowing rows for planting or grading roads for driving. They knew sacrifice and hard times. They survived and thrived on a strong faith in God and fierce determination, seasoned with the spice of good humor and a great love for kin and neighbor alike.

My grandmothers were strong of body and spirit, the backbone of the family, the glue that held things together. Grandmama Spicer was sweet and gentle, the storyteller and oral conveyor of family history and tall tales of strange folks and haunts; a baker of cat-head biscuits and an avid fisher-woman of catfish and bass, if she was able to cast far enough from the bank. Grandma Kelly was harder to take and more mischievous in nature; a born gossip and pot-stirrer if there ever was one. She would play the church organ on Sunday, then court controversy and conflict every other day of the week. My father once told me she was so rough in hide and disposition, that it would take a roll of sandpaper and a handful of tacks just to wipe her ass.

My grandfathers were hard-working, no-nonsense men; salt of the earth. Not that they didn't have their faults. There were plenty. Pappy Spicer could be rude and crude at times... a man who worked fluently in profanity the way some men did at woodworking or stone masonry. In his younger days he had been an itinerant farmer of tobacco and corn, working other men's land for a share of the crop and a place to live. Later he was a barber that had shorn many a scalp and shaved many a whisker in the back room of a general store. He was also a notorious drunkard – the town boozer – who had a nasty habit of blowing a week's pay on a night's worth of liquor. Later in life, he made his living trapping and selling furs, and digging wild ginseng from the woods, drying it on sheets of tin, and selling the medicinal root for a hefty price per pound.

My Grandpa Kelly was just as rambunctious, but in a more subtle way. He always had a colorful turn of a phrase and his opinions were sometimes large and hard to swallow. Tall, iron-jawed, and rawboned, Grandpa had been a farmer the first thirty years of his adult life and a backhoe driver for the State of Tennessee for the last thirty. He was tight with a dollar and a skinflint to beat all skinflints. Like many rural men who had grown up during the Great Depression, he carried a money roll in his pocket that would choke a Missouri mule, rather than entrust it to the local bank. But he hated to remove that rubber band and let it loose. I recall after my high school graduation, he took a roll of twenties and hundreds from his overall pocket and blessed me with a single five dollar bill, which was still a bitter pill to take for a man such as himself.

My father and mother were cut from the same cloth as those who had sired and birthed them, but were infinitely different in many ways. My father, Robert, was a quiet, easy-going man, but one with a timid streak; he avoided conflict and tended to duck it when he saw it coming, than face it head-on. I attribute much of this to his childhood, where his insecurities were cultivated by an older brother which his parents proudly proclaimed as "Son", much to his detriment, and an older, dominating sister who was every bit as sharp-tongued and trouble-making as their mother was. After graduating high school, Daddy joined the Army, serving four years in South Korea and four in Germany. He was in the same unit as Elvis Presley when he was there, but never laid eyes on the rock and roll legend (I'm sure the King was comfortably under wraps somewhere, and not subjected to peeling potatoes or cleaning latrines like the other GIs). After leaving the service, Daddy became a tool and die man and worked in the same shop for well over forty years.

My mother, Earline (or 'Nean' to her family) was a lot like my dad in some ways and completely different in others. Her childhood had been more difficult; stress and insecurity taxed her emotionally and something short of malnutrition inflicted her physically during her formative years, mostly due to her father's alcoholism. At the age of eight, she went to the creek for drinking water and was mercilessly swarmed by mosquitoes. Typhoid fever came soon afterward and she spent the better part of a year in a Nashville hospital, suffering from burning fevers and delirium, and making a slow recovery. It was at that time, that Mama developed an uncanny ability to foresee future events and predict forthcoming births and deaths. Grandmama called it her "second sight"... sort of a Tennessee version of "shining". Many refuse to believe in such things, but it happened with her time after time, with such frequency, that it proved to be much more than simply intuition on her part. When Mama turned fourteen, she left her home town and traveled to Nashville to work in the textile mills. She never told me, word for word, why she had felt the need to leave home at such an early age, but I gradually suspected that it had to do with family abuse of a sordid nature. I believe that this, along with her gift (or curse) of second sight, was the reason she suffered from severe depression and anxiety all of her life.

So... when did I come into the picture?

My mother and father met in Nashville, Tennessee in 1955. She was a production worker at the Werthan Bag Company. He was a young PFC home on furlough midway through a stint in Korea. My uncle, Al (afore mentioned as the spectacular "Son" of the Kelly clan), roomed in the same boarding house as my mom. The way Mama told it to me, Daddy was hot on her heels from the moment he laid eyes on her. "He was sort of like a big, goofy puppy dog," she said, "following me around, wouldn't leave me alone for a minute. So, I thought, if he's that crazy about me, I might as well marry the poor guy and get it over and done with."

They married at the courthouse in the town of Springfield, Tennessee (where, incidentally, my wife, Joyce, and I tied the knot), and, afterward, Daddy went back to Korea, while Mama quit her job and stayed home (like a new wife was expected to do in the mid-50s). When 1956 rolled around, Mama said she complained to Daddy about needing a way to get around town that didn't involve riding the bus. He sent her some money and told her to buy a car. Now, you must understand... the Kellys were a miserly bunch. It was a good bet that they had only bought used vehicles from the beginning of the Industrial Revolution and nothing else. So, imagine my father's shock and dismay when she wrote to him and told him that she had used that money as a down payment on a brand spanking-new, two-toned, 1956 Chevrolet Bel-Air. Apparently, he was so distraught that he sent Mama a telegram – not a letter, but a freaking telegram – conveying his displeasure at her expensive purchase. According to her account, she read the telegram, then promptly stuck it in her keepsake box and forgot all about it. When he finished his first tour of service and came home, he apparently forgot his outrage and fell in love with that two-tone Chevy. He owned it until 1972, when he traded it in for a Toyota Corolla station wagon.

Rather than stay in the States, get a job, and start a new life with his new wife, he chose to reenlist. This time he would be stationed in Germany (along with that invisible, pelvis-shaking boy from Memphis). This sort of pissed Mama off. She often told me that she thought Daddy did that "to avoid the responsibility of being a married man". She was probably right on that account. My mother was seven years older than Daddy, so she was a bit more mature than he was during that point in time.

Around February of 1959, Daddy came home on leave and I was conceived. When he discovered Mama was pregnant, he did his best to talk her into coming to Germany and living there, off base. She rejected the notion, though. "I knew I couldn't go," she told me once. "I had the strongest feeling that, if something bad happened during your delivery there, we would both die." As it turned out, her eerie powers of precognition was salvation for mother and child. There were severe complications during the delivery and both she and I came precariously near death. If we had been in an ill-equipped German hospital, instead of one with every modern advantage, we wouldn't have made it. And you wouldn't be holding this – or any book with my name on it at all – in your hands.

Mama named me Ronald after Ronald Reagan, who was her favorite actor at the time. For the first couple of years, we lived in a rental house in Dickson, a few miles from her hometown of White Bluff. Since it was just me and Mama, we developed a deep, personal bond from the very beginning (as I grew older, I came to realize that it was practically a *psychic* bond of sorts; when she was happy, so was I... when she was upset or depressed, ditto.). She said when Daddy was done with his Army days and came home for good, he walked in, decked out in his dress uniform, and handed me a toy bus (apparently a souvenir he'd bought at a Greyhound station during his journey home). After a few moments of glaring jealously, I walked over, handed him his hat, and said "Now... GO!" Daddy laughed and said, "You're not getting rid of me that easily, young man!"

Shortly afterward, Mama and Daddy moved back to the city and rented an old house on Elkins Avenue in West Nashville. Daddy got a job at Skyline Manufacturing as a tool and die worker, making a whopping forty bucks a week, while Mama played the homemaker role, this time with an actual husband in the picture.

Thus began the beginning of our happy little family.

Grits & Bits

Just do it!: Some folks never go to college or have a degree in English or literature, or have even taken Creative Writing classes. If you feel like you want or need to write, do it. You may be a grocery store clerk, a blue collar worker, or a farmer... but that doesn't mean that you can't cultivate the ability to move and motivate people with you words and ideas. Study what you read and learn by trial and error if that's what it takes. Don't let educational limitations build a wall between you and your literary aspirations.

Generating Empathy & Loathing: What truly drives a story? Plot? Setting? The final payoff at the end? True, all of those are necessary and important in making a story or novel an effective and involving piece of fiction. But, believe it or not, characterization is the main key. Without engaging and true-to-life characters to propel the storyline forward and bring it to satisfying fruition, a story is simply an idea with no meat on its bones.

Your characters – both protagonists and antagonists – must generate an emotional response in the reader. Empathy for the good guy and loathing for the bad guy is the traditional norm in horror literature (although past vampire tales have given the bloodsuckers more sympathy than abhorrence, via Anne Rice's *Vampire Chronicles* and Stephenie Myer's *Twilight* series.) I, myself, prefer the tried and true battle between good and evil, rather than leaving the tale in shades of gray that fail to favor one over the other.

Protagonists are the heroes of the story, battling the monster or evil that threatens or stands in their way. The reader must empathize with them to the point that they feel like a close friend or a dear family member. In turn, when they feel fear and horror, so do we. When they are hurt or fail to survive, we feel a loss akin to grief. I've been told that the final scene between Jeb Sweeny and Roscoe Ledbetter in my coming-of-age novel, *Fear*, has conjured tears and a feeling of genuine loss in those who have read it. That was not my original intention when I wrote the book, but, hey, I'll be happy to embrace that reaction. In my opinion, physical tears shed for the sake of a fictional character is one of the finest tributes to an author's work.

In turn, the antagonist – the villain of the story – should generate strong feelings of loathing, disgust, and, yes, pure hatred. *But what is their motivation for being so evil?* some readers tend to ask. *Why do they do the nasty things they do?* That's the old sympathy for the devil/murderer/monster/vampire enigma rearing its psychoanalytical head again. Sometimes evil is simply evil – there's no cause, only devastating effect. Sometimes folks just do evil things because they like to or they get off on it.

More often than not, successfully rendered characters beget a successfully executed piece of prose. Readers go to a particular piece of fiction to make an emotional investment. As the creator, do your best to provide a memorable experience... one that will stay with them long beyond the last paragraph.

Chapter Two

Four

W hen I was four years old, four pivotal things took place in my young life... things that made a lasting impression upon me and still affect me to this day.

One was the *scarring*. It happened one afternoon while my mother and I visited my aunt in the summer of 1963. Back then, folks drank a hell of a lot of coffee and, every time someone showed up on someone's doorstep, it was time to brew a fresh pot. In my Aunt Hazel's case, it was one of those tall chrome coffee percolators. The only outlet to plug it in was located on the other side of the doorway between the living room and kitchen. As Mama and her sister sat at the table and talked, I was playing-acting like I was a train. I don't recall why; maybe it was from a show I'd seen on the black-and-white TV or purely from my imagination. Anyway, as I drove the locomotive through the kitchen doorway I reached up with my hand to toot-toot the horn and, well, you know what happened then. I pulled the cord.

The next thing I remembered, I was lying on the floor and my mother was screaming at the top of her lungs. I didn't know it at the time, but the scalding contents of that toppling coffee pot had doused my left arm, barely missing my head by inches. After that, there was a frantic drive to the hospital in the '56 Chevy. I remember sea foam green walls, a 7UP machine, and a kindly doctor hovering over me, attending to my wound. I remember screaming for my mother and wailing "Let me go! Let me go!" (Many years later, this frightening episode would inspire my short story "Dead Skin".) After that, I remember my arm being bandaged from just below the shoulder to just above the wrist. I also remember a massive brown teddy bear that Mama and Daddy bought me and how I clung to that new friend like it was a life preserver. When the dressing was removed, there were several patches of ugly scar tissue on my bicep and forearm. I still have those scars (plastic surgery on children was practically unheard of in the early sixties and so none was ever performed), and while they are relatively small and insignificant now, as a small child the thick patches of malformed skin pretty much wrapped completely around my arm.

The scars were not pleasant to look at and drew stares from fellow children and adults alike. When I began school, they were akin to a badge of shame in my young mind. My peers either laughed and made fun of me, or were hesitant to even come near me, as though the scars might by transferred to their flesh by some form of close-contact leprosy. In turn, I felt as though I was an outcast... like damaged goods in a world of perfect, unblemished boys and girls. I carried that insecurity throughout my grade school years and even into high school. The only good thing to become of the scarring is that it taught me how to tell my left from my right. Even today, when my wife says turn left while I'm driving, I will look down at the scars to make sure I'm heading in the right direction.

The second thing that happened was that I learned to read and write. My mother was something of a progressive as far as believing that a child should begin learning early and amass basic knowledge and skills before they even entered kindergarten. Around the time that I was three years old, she bought me a small standing blackboard. This black board had Bugs Bunny at the upper left hand corner and Daffy Duck on the upper right hand. Printed in-between, was the alphabet and numbers printed in white. My mother said that I copied my letters and numbers over and over again, and, as I neared my fourth birthday, told her that I wanted to learn to read books. Although my fourth birthday party was vague in my memory, I do recall two gifts that I received. One was a wind-up toy robot that walked across the floor, lights blinking and flashing. The other was a copy of *Green Eggs & Ham* by Dr. Seuss. With Mama's help, I sounded out the words and, eventually, could read that book from cover to cover. The books that followed included more Seuss, Little Golden Books, the adventures of Curious George, and the anthropomorphic animal world of Richard Scarry. By the time I began kindergarten, I could read and write as well as any second-grader, which amazed and perplexed my teacher to no end.

The third had to do with faith and how it wasn't set in stone, like most folks believe. Grandma and Grandpa Kelly had come up to Nashville for a visit. Now this was a mighty rare thing, since they were rural homebodies and almost never left the farm in their Murray County hometown of Theta. Maybe they had come to see "Son" Al and stopped by Daddy's, out of obligation. I was too young to know or care about the reasons. Well, after supper, I played in the living room floor with bendable Gumby and Pokey and their bright yellow jeep, something I'd gotten for Christmas the year before. The folks came in and sat down and apparently Mama told Grandma that Daddy was no longer a Baptist, but was now a member of the Church of Christ. Well, that went over like gasoline on hemorrhoids. They squared off and then came the "Great Debate" as I have come to consider it.

Tennessee is the shiny gold buckle of the Southern Bible Belt, or it used to be. Not as many folks attend church or believe in Jesus as fervently or faithfully as they once did. The Kellys were always church-going people and so were the Spicers (Mama's side of the family), except for Pappy Spicer and a few of the uncles. So, it wasn't surprising that I was being raised in church. Most of what I remembered about it at that age was Vacation Bible School. There were the songs ("Deep and Wide", "Father Abraham", "I'm in the Lord's Army", and "The B-I-B-L-E", to name a few), as well as the customary snack of pineapple juice and Nilla Wafers afterward. Anyway, I was firmly anchored to the doctrine and practice of the denomination of the Church of Christ, mostly because in that era of the South the family usually gravitated toward the mother's choice of faith. And that meant that dear old Dad usually had to give in and join up too, if only to make Mama happy. And like they say, "If Mama ain't happy, ain't nobody happy."

Well, back to the "Great Debate". Grandma Kelly hadn't brought her Bible with her, but she had plenty of scripture ammunition loaded in her head and she was ready for bear. My mother was usually a quiet, meek woman, but when it came to her faith, she could be both adamant and relentless. Mama *did* have a Bible; a huge King James Version with a textured depiction of a Biblically-coiffed man – maybe Jesus? – gathering wheat in a field... bringing in the sheaves, so to speak. It was a cover that I loved as a child and I liked to lay a sheet of notebook paper across it and run a crayon across the image until it showed up in stark relief. Well, Mama took that big Bible off the coffee table and denominational theology, including bylaws and personal belief, was batted back in forth like a furious tennis match between two angry players... except that the ball that they were serving to one another was more like a hand grenade about to go off.

I remember sitting there on the living room rug, paralyzed in fear, as voices rose and faces grew livid and red. I looked around and Grandpa and Daddy were no longer there. I could see them through the screen of the front door, wanting no part of the turmoil inside. Grandpa had that wry grin on his face, for he knew how riled up Grandma could get when her religion was challenged. I grew terrified as tempers rose, as well as the voices behind them. I grabbed Gumby and Pokey and dove behind the sectional couch like a marine commando diving behind a stone wall before an enemy mortar could take him out.

I must have crouched there in the shadows for a good two hours... just me, Gumby, Pokey, and the dust bunnies. Doctrine and tradition were examined heatedly, with liberal bucketfuls of scripture being applied in a break-neck manner. Music in church versus only congregational singing. The Lord's Supper every Sunday or only quarterly. Once-saved-always-saved or the chance of losing one's salvation if you didn't follow the straight and narrow. Things I had never learned in Sunday School assaulted my tender ears like fiery meteors from Heaven raining down upon the sinful of Sodom and Gomorrah. I knew of Noah and the Ark, as well as Jonah in the Whale, but my teacher had never involved us in the "Great Debate" and it scared the living shit out of me.

Eventually, things settled down and it was called a draw. Mama returned the big KJV to the coffee table and

Grandma went home with Grandpa, sullied up and none too pleased. And it took Mama and Daddy a hysterical half hour of searching to find me, because I'd fallen asleep behind the couch and they couldn't find me.

I reckon what that terrifying episode taught me – and it was years later upon reflection, and not when I was crouching in the shadows protecting Gumby and Pokey from a hail of fire and brimstone – is that religion is not a cut-dried-subject. Folks who have faith in their box of life tools have all manner of opinions and preconceived notions about how God should be worshiped and how benevolent or judgmental He is. It's not justifiable for any of us to say who's right or wrong, whether someone's going to heaven or hell for doing or not doing a particular thing.

Now, on to number four. And, boy, was it a doozy.

November 22, 1963. What I remember about that day is hazy... just bits and pieces. I remember that me and Mama had lunch, and maybe I went down for a nap afterward. I remember Mama sitting on the couch, on the phone, crying. There were no cartoons on TV that afternoon, only the news. Everyone was sad. I asked if someone had died. Mama hugged me and said "Yes."

A couple of days passed. Everyone was distraught and on edge. Daddy came in after work, with a hard-edged grin on his face, and said "Someone shot the bastard!" I believe he was talking about Lee Harvey Oswald. I remember seeing a wagon on TV with an American flag draped over a long box and a little boy standing at attention, wearing short pants. I remember thinking *It's almost winter and this boy's legs are getting cold.*

I had a vague and disturbing feeling that things had changed from that point onward. At the age of four I had no idea that a President had been gunned down in Dallas or that his wife stood, in shock, shortly afterward, blood splattering her pink outfit, while another man took her husband's job. All I knew at that point was that it made my parents sad and angry, and, in turn, it made me feel that way, too. It was a dismal November, followed by a solemn December. I remember going Christmas shopping with my mom at a big department store downtown and all the salesmen were wearing black bands on their upper arms.

Years later, in grade school, when we studied the Assassination of John F. Kennedy, I began to realize that America wasn't Superman, no matter how many flags we waved or patriotic songs we sang in assembly. It wasn't bulletproof. Its pride could be bruised and its innocence stripped away in a matter of minutes. That we, as a country, could bleed and suffer. It has happened several times afterward during my lifetime. Vietnam, Watergate, 9/11, several periods of civil unrest, and recently with COVID-19. However, when you bleed and suffer, but you fail to die and give up the ghost, there's nothing more to do than get back up and keep going, like stubborn zombies in an old B horror movie. And hope and pray that the good times outweigh the bad.

Ten Books that Influenced and Changed Me as a Reader, Writer, and Person

1 *Green Eggs & Ham* by **Dr. Seuss** - The book that taught me how to read at the age of four. Despite the man's rejection and condemnation by today's 'literary police', the man paved the way to middle grade and young adult reading for my generation (and generations that followed), imparting a love for simplicity and rhythm, along with others like Richard Scarry, Margret and H.A. Rey, Shel Silverstein, and Roald Dahl.

2. *The Wonderful Wizard of Oz* by **L. Frank Baum** - The book that taught me that, in fiction, anything is possible, however implausible or unbelievable. It also gave some very eccentric characters (a scarecrow, a tin man, and a talking lion) license to romp through my imagination on a quest to return a lost child to her home once again.

3. *Charlotte's Web* **by E.B. White** - The book that taught me that animals can be more human than we are. It also taught me that dialogue and the execution of its rhythm can make a story gripping or enchanting, even if it is considered a children's book.

4. *Doc Savage* **by Kenneth Robson (Lester Dent)** - The series of books that gave me a voracious love of reading at the age of twelve and a love for time periods in fiction that were before my own. It also infused a writing style into my past and present prose; a style some label as "pulpy" or "shlocky"... sort of a common man's approach to spinning yarns. One that I don't deny or reject. One that has served me well throughout the years.

5. *To Kill A Mocking Bird* **by Harper Lee** - The book that had a profound emotional impact on me at the age of 16 and made me want to be a writer. My already mounting abhorrence to racial injustice – as a child, an adolescent, and teen moving toward manhood – solidified with Lee's book. It showed me how very cruel, destructive, and utterly pointless racism really was and opened my eyes to what was going on around me, and had been for some time.

6. *Salem's Lot* **by Stephen King** - The book that showed me exactly what genre I wanted to write in. My first experience with King showed me that it was okay to be weird, to love horror and write about it. Both the book and the TV mini-series left terrifying impressions that were both disturbing and deliciously welcome to an introverted boy who was sometime persecuted for showing interest in such stuff.

7. *The Holy Bible*, **the inspired Word of God** - Say what you will, ridicule or embrace it... but for me, this will always be THE book; the foundation of my faith and the source of my hope and joy. (It also contains some great horror stories!)

8. *Boy's Life* **by Robert McCammon** - My all-time favorite coming-of-age novel and a book that showed me that a writer from the South could make it in this business. The ease of McCammon's storytelling showed me that it was better to draw from the well of solid characterization and chapter-by-chapter vignettes, than to try to impress readers with lofty prose and literary pomp.

9. *Midnight Rain* **by James Newman** - One of the first novels I read after a long ten-year hiatus from writing or reading horror fiction, and the one that inspired me to return to the genre. Like McCammon, Newman shoots from the hip with no grandstanding bullshit, crafting dark tales that are customarily more crime/suspense than actual horror.

10. *The Memory Tree* **by John R. Little** - A novel I read at a very crucial time as a father, when I discovered that one off my children had been sexually abused at the age of six. It helped me through a particularly tough time that I would never want to experience again; a time when I thought that I had failed as a father, because I hadn't been able to identify certain signs and situations, and keep my precious child from trauma and harm. It also taught me that, no matter how much you'd like to turn back the hands of time, such a thing is impossible and that events cannot be undone.

Chapter Three

City Life

I have very distinct memories of life on the west side of Nashville as a young child. Even now I can picture the street we lived on – Elkins Avenue – as well as the various houses along the avenue and the folks who lived in them. Elderly Mrs. Abrams next door and, across the street, the Whitfield and Wix families. It might seem strange that I would even recollect very much about life on Elkin's Avenue at all, given that I was only between the ages of three and six, but I do.

The house we lived in was old; built in the 1930s. It was white clapboard with six rooms; living room, two bedrooms, a bathroom, dining room, and kitchen. Hardwood floors throughout; clean, but rundown. We rented it for forty dollars a month. Daddy was making forty a week back then in the early 60s, so rent took an entire week of his paycheck. It had a high porch on the back with no railing, so Mama wouldn't let me go out there by myself, because she was afraid I'd fall off and break my neck. We had a little back yard with a metal swing set and a hutch for a pet rabbit.

Our bunny was named Dutchie and he was black and white in color. Rabbits were acceptable pets back then; almost as much as a dog or cat is now. Around Easter, the five and dime store over on Charlotte Avenue would sell bunnies and folks bought them for the kids' Easter baskets. They also sold baby chicks and ducks, dyed bright pink, blue, green, and yellow and displayed them under a heat lamp in the front window of the store. These days, such haphazard commerce would be considered animal cruelty, but back then it was commonplace. Dozens upon dozens of little critters were sold as novelty items for the holidays with about as much regard as pumpkins at Halloween or fireworks on the Fourth of July.

The one thing I remember most about the old house on Elkin's Avenue was the basement. The cellar door stood in a small hallway between my bedroom and the dining room; a somber, heavy, wooden door painted black. I was absolutely terrified of that door and what might lurk behind it. Daddy would tell me ghost stories sometimes, like Bloody Bones or the ghost of a man with an arm of pure gold that had been killed for his valuable appendage. Mama was good at telling spooky tales, too, and often spoke of the Bell Witch, who haunted a cave up in Adams, Tennessee. At the age of four or five, I was completely convinced that all three – Bloody Bones, the Man with the Golden Arm, and the Bell Witch were congregating down in the dark pit of that basement, planning the best way to abduce a frightened, little boy and carry him, kicking and screaming, to their shadowy lair while is parents slept soundly. Some nights I would lie in my western wagon wheel twin bed and hear a scratching on the other side of the plaster wall, where the pitch black stairs of the cellar descended on the other side, and I knew they were coming for me. But it was only a mouse – or maybe even a rat – and I remained safely, head beneath covers, in my bed without the possibility of my face gracing the back of a milk carton.

My brother, Kevin, came along in March of 1964, when I was four and half years old. A little, rambunctious young'un that had been blessed with the fiery red hair of the Spicer's Scotch-Irish heritage (I myself had inherited the dark hair of my father and my Grandma Kelly's Shepherd kin.) Both my grandmothers claimed Cherokee in their bloodline, while my grandfathers were both red-headed and rawboned and as Irish in looks as they were redneck in nature. I remember feeling a little jealous of my new baby brother. After all, up until that point, I was the only kid in the household and was the center of my mother's attention. Now there was sibling competition to contend with. I wasn't exactly resentful of him being there; just a little apprehensive about how his presence would alter Mama's affections for me. Mama was a fair-minded parent, though. She loved both her boys equally, and soon my fears were soothed. I looked forward to the day when my brother would be old enough to play with Matchbox cars and G.I. Joes, wrestle in the grass, and ride with me on the backseat of the '56 Chevy, where we would get in petulant shouting matches over one or the other touching or staring at each other (as we invaded each other's personal space) between annoying cat-calls of "Are we there yet?" or "I gotta pee... real bad!"

I recall summers on Elkins Avenue. Daddy and Mrs. Abrams (who was like a surrogate granny) mowing the grass with their four-blade push reel lawn mowers (the kind with no engine; just elbow grease and muscle to chop away that stubborn Johnson grass). I also remember the popsicle man coming around daily (you might have called them the 'ice cream man' where you come from, but down here in the South they're the 'popsicle man'). Mama always had a dime handy and, when I heard that off-key popsicle truck music wailing from a block down the street, I'd run out and meet him at the sidewalk. Blue Boys and Firecrackers (the red, white, and blue ones) were my favorites. Sometimes Mama would get a hankering and send me with an extra dime for an ice cream sandwich. I recall that Kevin was partial to orange push-ups and Mama would sit him in his steel throne of a highchair, stripped to the cloth diaper, and let him go at it full force. Before he was done, he looked like a bright orange Pillsbury doughboy from head to toe.

Christmas was a special time in West Nashville. We would drive downtown on the weekends and see Santa at Harvey's Department Store or go out to Centennial Park and view the annual Nativity display in front of the full-scale replica of the Greek Parthenon. I always asked for G.I. Joes (this was the era of the foot-long Joes, not the three-and-a-half inchers), as well as an occasional battery-powered robot or monster-themed toy. And, of course, Batman merchandise was always welcome from Santa's sack. Our Christmas tree was the old silver aluminum kind with the color wheel that changed it different colors as the disc spun and the big bulb behind it cast its rainbow glow. Kevin and I would lay on the living room floor for hours, just watching that metallic tree change from red to blue to green to yellow. Today's children would watch this agonizingly slow transition of primary hues and be bored silly in thirty seconds. Back then, it didn't take much to entertain us. We didn't have Xbox or cell phones or brain-numbing tomfoolery on Tic-Toc, so our attention spans were longer and more satisfying.

I remember when I was five, Mama had a particularly frightening episode of premonition. I was sitting at the kitchen table, working fervently at a coloring book (Flintstones, Woody Woodpecker, Jetsons?), waiting for my favorite breakfast delicacy; scrambled eggs with ketchup. Mama was standing at the stove, preparing to whop a can of biscuits against the edge of the kitchen counter. The can slipped from her hand and fell on the head of our dog, a fuzzy white and brown terrier named Chipper. At the very moment that happened, she saw my uncle John A being crushed beneath an overturned truck. This devastated her and she waited, pale and withdraw, for two weeks until it actually happened and her brother was killed in a violent head-on collision.

This wasn't the first time Mama had predicted tragedy in the family. Early one Saturday morning in 1950, my grandmother had answered her door to find my mother standing there, clearly agitated. This surprised Grandmama, because Mama had been working in Nashville and she hadn't seen her for several weeks. Mama urged her to get dressed... that they were going back to Nashville on the bus for the day. Grandmama once told me that she did as she asked because she knew by the look on Mama's face that she had *sensed* that something bad was going to happen and knew not to take her daughter's premonitions lightly. They went to Nashville and shopped, had lunch, and then got back on the bus. When they returned to the little town of White Bluff that evening, they discovered what had happened. Like Pappy Spicer in his wilder days, some of my uncles were prone to drink. They were the kindest and friendliest guys imaginable... until they got liquored up. Then they turned vindictive and mean. Grandmama once told me, when Pappy was barbering, she'd have to hide the tools of his trade when the boys got drunk or they'd go at each other with shaving strops and straight razors. Anyway, on that fateful day in 1950, two of my uncles, Ward and Rance, had indulged in the bottle and matters had deteriorated swiftly. Ward had started making fun of Rance (who had once suffered a severe heatstroke in Army boot camp and was mentally-challenged because of it) and shoved him off the porch of the house. Rance, in turn, walked into the house, retrieved a twelve-gauge shotgun, and blew Ward in half with both barrels. Mama later told me that she had known something awful was in store for a member of her family, but didn't know which one; that she had had a nightmare a week or so before about a tombstone that bore no name at the head of a freshly-dug grave in the town cemetery. The details of what happened afterward are a little sketchy in my mind, since no one in the family really wanted to dwell on that awful incident. The truth of the matter was, Uncle Ward, who I never had the pleasure to meet, was dead, and Uncle Rance had been sent to prison for a long stretch. Perhaps he didn't spend the rest of his life there because of his mental state and the fact that he was inebriated at the time. After his release, he lived at home with Grandmama and Pappy; spending his days drinking coffee on the front porch swing, hunting or fishing, or whittling and listening to Johnny Cash and George Jones on his AM radio.

So, back to Elkins Avenue. When I was five, Mama enrolled me in kindergarten. I remember getting up for school in the morning, watching a half hour of the Three Stooges or Little Rascals as I ate breakfast, and then walking the block to Park Avenue Elementary School. The school was located on the next street over and Mama could stand on the back porch and make sure I safely reached my destination if I crossed through the back yards and the school playground. Park Avenue School was a two-story, red brick institution with the lower grades on the ground floor and the upper grades on top. I remembered that it reeked of tempera paint, white paste, and mimeograph ink, and that the gymnasium was our patriotic headquarters (a civic staple in that day and age) where we recited the Pledge of Allegiance and sang songs like "God Bless America" and "This Land is Your Land". It was the place where I had made my first best friend (the neighbor boy across the street, Roger Wix) and got my first crush on a girl in my class (Sandra by name). I remember walking up to Sandra in the lunch line one afternoon and telling her that we were going to be married and have lots and lots of babies. She promptly slapped me across the face. I attribute this incident with making me "girl shy" and stunting me socially for many years afterward.

One thing took place during first grade that disturbed me and troubled my mother to no end. One sunny morning, they herded all the students in the school onto bright yellow buses and drove us across town. When we reached another school (a dark and alien place to us frightened first-graders), we disembarked and were marched inside. All of us, boys and girls alike, were made to disrobe except for our underwear and we were physically examined, then giving a shot with one of those metal inoculation guns in the left arm. After that, we put on our clothes, got back on the bus, and went back to our own school.

My mother knew nothing about this until my arm started aching a day or two later; so badly that I cried almost constantly and couldn't sleep. She took me to the pediatrician, who informed her that I had been given an unknown shot... against her consent.

Now, you've got to understand something about my mother. She was a quiet, soft-spoken Christian woman, but she had a temper. If she got particularly riled up, she was like a Tasmanian devil with a splash of Louisiana hot sauce on its tonsils and a flame thrower up its ass. When she was thirteen, a boy in her class had pinched her breast and she had taken a wooden chair upside his head and knocked him senseless for three days. Pappy once told me that when he was cutting hair, he prayed for the Saturday mornings when that boy's father would come in for a trim and he had him trapped in his chair, so he could pester and pick at him about his daughter "laying that damn fool boy of yours out colder than a mud-sucking catfish for three days straight".

So, you can imagine what happened when she found out about that clandestine trip across town and the medicine of unknown origin that had pumped into my little arm. She went ballistic. From what she told me, she went to the school and the school board, and even higher ups (short of the Governor) trying to find out what sort of injection I had been subjected to without her knowledge. And, in turn, everyone she went to for answers denied that that morning trip on the bus had ever taken place. "It was just his imagination," they told her. "You know how little boys are." But neighbors with kids had also related similar stories, so she knew that I wasn't just making it up. As it turned out, my arm gradually got back to normal and Mama never did find out what it was in that mystery shot.

Sometimes, I think about it and wonder if I was subjected to some secret government experiment of Weird Science proportions. Who knows? Maybe I'll wake up one morning with an extra head or hair growing out of the soles of my feet or sporting super powers like "Flame On!" or X-Ray vision.

Grits & Bits

Editing as you go: Writers have different methods of how they tackle the grueling task of editing and polishing their work. Currently, a common practice seems to be submitting your story or novella to several beta readers for critical feedback, then doing a final edit or two (or more) afterward. To shorten the process, it may be better and more efficient to edit your work as you go. After you have written a page or two, go back and edit what you have done. When you reach the halfway point, go back and do it again, continuing to polish and refine. At the completion of the piece, go back and really give it thorough going-over, checking for grammar and punctuation mistakes, plot and a character inconsistencies, and areas that lag and slow the pace of the narrative (perhaps with needless dialogue or over description of characters and settings). A story or novel is like a garden; despite how good you believe it is in your 'writer's mind', there are always weeds to eradicate and bugs to exterminate.

Finding your literary voice: Face it, if we all wrote like Stephen King and set our fiction in the same fictional locales as he does, readers would be bored out of their skulls. Everyone should strive to find that special element (or combination of elements) that distinguishes their work from that of others. Want to write extreme horror? Fine...just don't do it the same way as Wrath James White, Aaron Beauregard, Edward Lee, or Jack Ketchum. Interested in penning stories with LGBTQ themes and characters? Great... simply try to avoid emulating Hailey Piper, Eric Larocca, or Aaron Dries. Work toward developing your own individual style and voice. It can be done with characters, settings, and mood, or snappy dialogue and humor. Take Joe Lansdale for example. You could read a story of his with no byline identifying the author and you would still know it was him. His unique prose and delivery just sort of unzips you, climbs inside, and walks around in your skin during the course of the narrative. Try to do the same... but on your own terms, with your own individual set of skills and literary dynamic.

Chapter Four

Country Life

Two weeks after I started the second grade at Park Avenue, we pulled up stakes and moved to the country.

This was not unexpected, but it still hit me sort of hard. I knew that Daddy had bought some land in a neighborhood in the little, rural town of Pegram and that we were building a house there. We would take the seventeen mile drive from Davidson County to Cheatham County on the weekends, and Mama and Daddy would take a look at the progress that the contractor, the Jones Company (still in business after 90 years), had made on the site during the previous week. But, I reckon it never really sank in that we were actually leaving Nashville, until Daddy backed the big Skyline Manufacturing truck from work into the driveway and he and some fellow coworkers started hauling out furniture and appliances.

Plainly put, I didn't want to go. Everything I'd known since the age of two had been based in the Sylvan Heights community of West Nashville. My dentist, my doctor, my school, my best friend, Roger, my favorite parks and stores, my day to day routine... all were centered there, firmly and comfortably. Ripping me away from all that familiarity and casting me into the rural unknown was frightening.

Pegram was a small town nestled in a valley surrounded by high, wooded hills on three sides and Highway 70 and railroad tracks on the fourth. There wasn't much to it, really. Two or three churches and a strip mall with the post office, a grocery store, and a bank. A gas station next to that and, down the highway a piece, a couple more country stores with gas pumps. There was an elementary school and, as it turned out, it was located directly behind my neighborhood, so I had the convenience of walking down my backyard, crossing a railroad tie over a drainage ditch, and I was there. No riding the school bus; at least not until my high school years.

The new house was on Sunnyfield Drive. On one side were older houses, built in the 1940s and 50s, while on the other side was open, empty acreage. That's where we built our house. It was a three-bedroom ranch-style with red brick and white trim. Cedar-paneled combination dining room and kitchen, small bathroom with sea foam green tile, and an attached garage. The living room had Spanish style furniture; all black vinyl, dark wood, and burgundy accents. Wrought iron wall hangings and pictures of bullfighters and Flamenco dancers. The kitchen had colored appliances. That was big during the 60s and 70s; refrigerators and stoves of harvest gold and avocado green. Ours was Coppertone.

I had trouble sleeping in the new house the first week we moved in. It was too clean and too quiet. No groaning or popping or settling of old, weathered boards. No nocturnal scratching on the other side of the bedroom wall. This house had no cellar, only a crawlspace underneath. I lay in the top bunk of mine and Kevin's bunk bed and thought of Bloody Bones, Golden Arm, and the Bell Witch and wondered if they still haunted the old house, maybe lonesome and playing Go Fish or Candyland. Maybe they even missed me and their thwarted plan for my nocturnal abduction.

School at Pegram Elementary was harder than it had been in Nashville. First of all, they were much more advanced in math, my absolute worst subject. Where I had been doing addition and subtraction at my old school, my new school was already heavily into multiplication and division. I had a difficult time wrapping my head around long division and it was frustrating to the point of terrifying. The teachers were kind and understanding, but I struggled that first year in trying to sync myself with the curriculum.

There were two other things that I struggled with as well. One was bullying. I didn't remember being bullied or victimized at the school in Nashville, but it came to me full force at my new one. I've always been short in stature; it was a hereditary trait from my mother's side of the family, and I was always the smallest boy in my class, even halfway through high school. Therefore, I got picked on a lot. Size had much to do with it, but it was also because I was an outsider. That's how it is in rural communities. If you were born and raised there, if you possess one of the local *names*, you are accepted and life goes smoothly. If you're not, if you're the new kid from – heaven forbid, another *county*! – you had to bust your ass to prove yourself or fight to fit in. It is still that way today in small rural towns. You can manage to fit in and ingratiate yourself with the populace if you are good at sports and your parents are gung-ho sports parents. But, for those of us who aren't – those who would rather draw a picture or read a book than shoot the hoops or run a touchdown – we're the weird ones... the misfits, the outsiders.

Another thing that became very clear to me in my hometown was racism. Now, I'm not saying this particular town was any more racist than any other place I've lived. I guess at the age of seven, it was just more apparent there than it had been in my neighborhood in Nashville. And maybe it was the first time in my life that I sensed that the scales weren't evenly balanced as far as how folks of different races were perceived and treated.

Now, this is the part of the book where I'm bound to piss off some folks I grew up with in a mighty big way. However, if I sugar-coat or ignore how things were back then, then I'm not being completely honest. And, if I choose to take that road, then there's no justification in me writing this Southern-Fried memoir in the first place. Some folks will call me a liar and claim it never happened... but I'm not and it did. So, here it goes.

About a mile from my house was a tall hill where all the black families lived. As far as I know, everyone in town referred to it as N---r Hill. It was an extremely impoverished community, with ramshackle houses and trailers with junk and the rusty hulls of cars in the yards out front. The road that ran through it was a dirt one; it wasn't paved like the ones down in town, not back in 1967 at least. In fact, the town dump was located at end of the road that wound through the Hill and the stench of rotten food and garbage permeated the place for a mile around. I remember riding to the dump with Daddy in the '56 Chevy and, even in the sweltering heat of summer, the car windows would be rolled up and the doors locked.

All right... let's step away here for a moment and let me say a few things about Daddy. My father was a kind, loving, hardworking man. He was a churchgoer and a good husband and father to his family. But he had his flaws and one of them was his prejudice against folks of a different color (here is where I'm liable to piss off some family as well, so Ol' Ron is wading in hot water up to his nipples now.) He liked to poke fun at and make off-color jokes about blacks; not to their face, but at home and around his coworkers. This exasperated Mama something awful and, later, when I was in my teens and early twenties, it infuriated me to no end. I hate to come right out and say that he was actually racist, because I knew the man and I don't believe he had a hateful, vindictive bone in his body. Rather, I think he had been conditioned since his formative years to think and act in such a way by the folks he had been raised by, and such behavior had become second-nature to him. He was also taught, I believe, to fear and distrust those different than he was, mostly by my conservatively-opinioned Grandpa Kelly. This doesn't excuse what Daddy said or thought or why he acted in the way that he did, but I think it partly explains it. I loved my father dearly and his prejudices did soften in his later years, but he never did quite come to the realization that all folks, no matter what gender or race or orientation they might be, are equal in the sight of God (a fact that my mother believed to be true from the very beginning).

Okay, then... let's go back to town again. My elementary school only had a handful of black children. Almost all of them were separated into a different section of the same class. The school system claimed that it was because they were "slow" (today's equivalent of special education). As I grew older, it seemed more like segregation in reflection. When on the playground for recess, black and white students pretty much kept to their own private groups. Maybe out of a form of self-segregation? More than likely because their parents had suggested that it would be better that way.

The unfairness of it all came more brilliantly to light during the holidays. On Valentine's Day we made shoeboxes decorated with colored hearts with a slit in the lid for valentines (not the one-piece kind we have today, but the kind in their own individual envelopes with your beloved's name scrawled on the front.) It was a safe bet (and an unspoken code) that no white kids would be depositing valentines in a black kid's box. My mother wouldn't allow it, though. She had me make valentines for every student in the class. "They're as deserving as you are," she told me. "Maybe more so". So, the next day, I took my valentines and made my rounds among the decorated boxes on the classroom desks. And, being as discreet as possible (so as not to garner the wrath of the bullies who already tormented me), I would slip the 'special' valentines into the right boxes... the ones that Mama had slipped a sucker or a couple of pieces of bubble gum inside the envelope. Years later, while standing in line in a grocery store, one of those classmates, perhaps thirty in age, turned to me and said "Thanks for that valentine in third grade. You didn't have to do it, but you did. So, thank you."

However, there was one incident that bothered me more than all the rest, and it still comes uncomfortably to mind, even after all these years. It was at a school assembly. Each class was to put on a skit or sing a song. Our class decided to sing a song, while one of the students acted it out on stage. Our song? "Old Black Joe". They picked one of the boys of color from the class to be the title character; for the sake of discretion, we'll just say his name was "Bill". So... the song. A Stephen Foster tune written in 1853. About an elderly slave from the "cotton fields" who laments sorrowfully about the old days when he was "young and gay" (take a moment to Google the lyrics and give it a read. It'll likely put your blood to boiling). Anyway, they dressed Bill up in shabby old clothes, powdered his hair white with baking flower, gave him a cane, and had him shuffle (that was the teacher's suggestion, not a word of my own choosing) across the stage floor from one curtain to another. And all the while, my class was belting out "Old Black Joe" to the laughter and amusement of the audience who sat in the bleachers of the gym. If a child of color were to be subjected to such a spectacle today, it's safe to say that the outrage would be of international proportions. But it happened back then and no one said a word... and it was called entertainment.

Another incident of a racial nature happened when I was eight years old. I've told this story before in my Halloween collection, *Mister Glow-Bones*, but I'll tell it again here, since it impacted me in a very disturbing and lasting way.

1968 was a very dark and dangerous time, not only in my hometown, but across the nation. During April of that year, Martin Luther King had been assassinated at the Lorraine Motel in Memphis and, in turn, people we had never seen as much of a threat now seemed to possess the potential to be so. Animosity between the races was building at a steady pace and it seemed like only a matter of time before hostile feelings got the better of reason, in both whites and blacks.

That Halloween night had a different feeling to it. There was a blanket of tension over the entire community and particularly in the faces of my mother and father. My parents forbid us to stray beyond the stretch of our street, but wouldn't give us a concrete explanation why that restriction had been set. Still, we netted a bagful of Halloween candy by eight o'clock. As was customary, my brother and I would don our pajamas by eight-thirty and begin the task of separating our treasure trove of treats into separate piles: bubble gum, suckers, candy bars, etc.

It was nearing nine o'clock when the worst fears of our hometown almost came true... within our own home.

Someone knocked on our door and, being the trusting lady she was, my mother went to answer it. As I arranged my candy, I heard her say "What do you want?" and then, in growing alarm, "You can't come in here!" I turned and looked through the doorway that lay between the living room and the dining room. There were six or seven tall, young black men entering the house, silently, but deliberately. They said nothing at all. They simply walked in, carrying the smell of autumn wood smoke and damp leaves with them. Two of them were actually through the doorway and in the dining room, when my father's voice boomed from the end of the hallway near the bathroom. "What are you doing here?"

That was when the invaders lost their nerve. They scrambled for the door, afraid that my father was about to shoot at them (which was impossible, since my mother forbid firearms in our house). I remember the last one – a boy no more than thirteen or fourteen years of age – turning and looking at me full in the face. There was as much fear in his eyes as there was in mine. But, before leaving, he couldn't resist grabbing up a handful of my very best candy; Babe Ruths, Butterfingers, and Tootsie Rolls. Then he was out in the darkness and running with the others.

I remember my mother sitting on the couch, her face pale with shock and fear, while my father stood in the yard ranting and raving. I also remember feeling anger at the theft of my candy bars. My brother, Kevin, only four at the time, didn't seem to realize the potential danger we had been in that night.

Many Halloweens have passed since then and now I can look back at 1968 objectively, with neither anger nor fear, but with understanding. At the age of eight, I knew nothing of the impact Martin Luther King had made upon the African-American community or the anger and loss they had experienced following his brutal killing.

But now, more than five decades later, I understand what they might have felt that year, when a smirking white face might have looked hauntingly like James Earl Ray to them and stirred feelings they wouldn't have normally even considered, let alone acted upon.

As for my stolen candy, I can't honestly begrudge that frightened teenager his clutching handful of Snickers and Bit-O-Honeys. I figure it may have been well-deserved, considering that he was restricted from trick-or-treating in my neck of the woods; barred from my picturesque Southern street by long-standing prejudice and underlying fear.

Of course, not everything during my early years in the town Pegram was grim and eye-opening. There were good times as well. Plenty of them.

My favorite teacher at Pegram Elementary was Mrs. Christine Harris. She was my fifth grade teacher and, when the sixth grade class was split in half due to size, I spent the following year with her as well. Mrs. Harris was kind, understanding, and just plain fun to be around. She was about the age of my Grandmama Spicer at the time, but there was a sparkle of youth and humor in her eyes that would put you to ease during the most difficult math test. I remember she wore her cats-eye glasses on a gold chain around her neck and her white sweater across her shoulders like the coronary cape of a queen.

From the age of six to twelve, I suffered painful ear infections every December like clockwork. Mama tried her best to prevent them, even buying me an earflap cap to protect me from the cold in the winter, but nothing seemed to help. This was before doctors started putting drainage tubes in kids' ears, so about all you could do was drink a gallon of that nasty pink medicine and wait it out. Most years, I was stuck at home, suffering from the infections, and not even at school when the class Christmas party rolled around.

The year of the fifth grade, Mrs. Harris showed up at our front door one evening with a Christmas gift in hand. As it turned out, she had bought every boy in class a three-bladed pocket knife. Now days, any teacher with the nerve of purchasing a potential weapon for a student would lose their teaching license and never grace the classroom again. But this was 1970 and I was ten years old and it was acceptable for a boy my age to have his own pocket knife. Some of the boys in my class even had BB guns or actual .22 rifles for hunting at that age, but I was never that fortunate, given my mother's aversion to firearms.

Anyway, Mama told me to be careful opening it... that it was liable to be sharp. She was right. I unfolded the first blade and promptly sliced the ball of my thumb wide open. Mama sprayed a little Bactine (the cure-all medicine of my childhood) on the cut, bandaged it, and, gently taking the knife, said "Let me put this away for you... until you think you're ready for it." As it turned out, I never asked for it back or even remember what became of it. In fact, I was "knife-shy" for a long time after that, or at least until my twenties when I would collect and even make knives myself.

Another thing I remember about those years were the toys. There were always G.I. Joes in the house and beneath the tree on Christmas morning. These were the big twelve-inch Joes with military clothing and vehicles like jeeps with spotlights and bazookas. Later, when Mattel gravitated away from the unsavory military stigma conjured by the Vietnam War, Joe became an adventurer. He sported realistic hair and beard, possessed the deadly Kung Fu Grip, and went in search of mummies and pigmy gorillas, instead of enemy soldiers.

There was just something about action figures that sparked my imagination between the age of six to ten. Captain Action and Doctor Evil, Major Matt Mason, Action Jackson, the Mego superheroes, and the thick plastic Marx figures – Johnny West, Sam Cobra, Chief Cherokee – that were so heavy you could have bludgeoned someone senseless with one.

One of my favorite toys was the Strange Change Time Machine from Mattel, which was basically a hot plate with a plastic dome chamber on top of it. You would plug it in, place one of the polyethylene "shape memory" time capsules on the heated grid, and they would magically unfold into creatures from another time or dimension: monsters, skeletons, aliens, insects, and dinosaurs. Then you would heat them back up, chuck them into the "compressor," a hand-cranked screw-press for returning the figures to their original flat, time capsule state. When the toy was officially recalled for being a "burning hazard", Mama forbid me from plugging the thing in. Nevertheless, my brother and I still made good use of the compressor, inserting Matchbox or Hot Wheel cars into the chamber and crushing them like they did at the big junkyard in Nashville.

I always had an obsessive interest in stuff like that. Weird and odd toys, television shows, and movies. Dinosaurs, robots, aliens, creepy-crawlers ...anything bizarre and beyond the norm. But, monsters... monsters were what enthralled and interested me the most.

And, so, that was where it all really began.

Grits & Bits

S **uspension of disbelief:** How does a writer of horror (or science fiction or fantasy) pull off supernatural and otherworldly storylines? How do they get their readers to accept wholeheartedly or "buy into" tales of vampires, werewolves, aliens, etc.?

I don't believe it has to do with the monster at all, no matter how well it is described or portrayed. The burden of belief rests on the shoulders of the main characters. If they react convincingly, like real-life people would if facing some creature beyond normal comprehension, that is where the barrier of disbelief breaks down. If your most skeptical character slowly comes to the dreadful realization that the threat is real and palatable – be it a backwoods vampire, an Irish werewolf, or a snake-critter from an evil county – and faces the threat as a flesh and blood person would, that is when suspension of disbelief becomes possible.

If your characters act and react implausibly or foolishly (like those silly teenagers in most of the slasher movies) then your creature might as well stay hidden in the shadows and remain the urban legend that the unbelieving think it is. The fear and emotion of your protagonists give the vampire its fangs and the lycanthrope its claws. Without that in its favor, the beastly antagonist – and your book or story—has no chance at all.

Chapter Five

The Little Boy Who Loved Monsters

When folks ask me that writer's question, you know, "How did you get into horror in the first place?", I like to tell a little story. Now, most of you who have listened to enough podcasts or read enough interviews know exactly what story it is. And you're probably rolling your eyes and thinking "Aww, here he goes again!" Well, since it's my story and maybe some of you *haven't* heard it... here I go again.

When my mother was pregnant with me, she moved away from Nashville, back to her hometown of White Bluff while my father was in Europe. She rented a little house where she intended to stay until Daddy came home from the service. Well, one afternoon, she climbed up into the attic to store a couple of boxes and discovered a whole stack of EC Horror comics. Tales from the Crypt, Vault of Horror, Haunt of Fear,

Crime SuspenStories. Now, this was early 1959, so it was safe to say that they'd probably been up there for nearly ten years. Having an interest in spooky stories and the macabre, Mama brought those comic books down and read them the entire time she was pregnant with me. So, while some kids got read fairy tales and Bible stories while floating in the birth chamber, I was being fed a steady diet of grave-bursting zombies, flesh-eating monsters, and crazed axe murderers.

I like to think that's why I gravitated to ghosts, werewolves, vampires and such from the very beginning. You may not believe that a baby can absorb vocal stories, books, and music while in the womb, but I do. I remember my wife and I read *One Hundred and One Dalmatians* to our oldest daughter, Reilly, before she was born. Since we also read *The Wizard of Oz* and *Charlotte's Web*, I always considered *Dalmatians* a peculiar and boring distant third (Cruella had a husband and the dogs did weird things, like hand-building carts and hauling each other around it them). Anyway, years later, after Reilly had watched Disney's cartoon adaptation, she said "Daddy... the movie is better than the book." But, of course, she had never read the book... we had.

Even as a very small child, I loved weird and frightening things. Particularly after starting grade school, my infatuation with Halloween and monsters seem to take a firm hold and that was what most of my thoughts and interests seemed to revolve around. I took to drawing when I was five or six and, at first, the sketches were minimally detailed and crude, exploring ghosts tales I'd heard or things I'd seen on television: the flying monkeys from Oz, the Loch Ness Monsters, the specter-like man in search of his golden arm, and, of course, Ol' Bloody Bones.

My infatuation with cinematic monsters began when I was six years old.

Up until then, my television viewing consisted mostly of Captain Kangaroo, Romper Room, and The Bozo the Clown Show (which was sort of like Pennywise with ADHD on methamphetamine). That and Saturday morning cartoons; you know, The Flintstones, Bugs Bunny, Mighty Mouse, and Popeye. Eventually, in the late 60s and early 70s, there would be better stuff: Scooby Doo, Space Ghost, Johnny Quest, The Herculoids, and manic psychedelic live-action shows like H.R. Puffenstuff and The Banana Splits.

When I started first grade, a show came on at three o'clock in the afternoon called The Big Show. It was local and hosted by Nashville Channel 5's handsome weatherman, Bob Lobertini. The Big Show featured every Universal Monster movie and 1950s giant atomic monster flick that you could imagine. Since we lived next to the school, I would run like a scalded hog to get home just in time to plop down on the couch before the show started. Baking was Mama's culinary specialty and she always had chocolate chip cookies, a piece of cake, or a slice of pie, and a cold glass of milk ready for me.

The first monster movie I ever watched was *The Creature from the Black Lagoon.* It both horrified and fascinated me. Just the opening scene – the Gillman's clawed hand reaching thorough the tent flap and grabbing that guy's face – told me that this was something entirely different than The Three Stooges or Rocky and Bullwinkle. I mean, this was a primordial missing link in the Amazon jungle, flaying the flesh off a screaming man's skull. So, naturally, I was hooked. And it also provided me with my first "full-grown woman" crush with swimsuit-clad Julie Adams. Now, you remember Sandra and what had happened to me back in kindergarten. After that humiliating incident, I had wanted nothing more to do with the female race, until Julie started back-stroking in the Black Lagoon. Good thing she escaped the Creature at the end of the movie. Can you imagine what sort of freaky kids they would have spawned?

Knowing that I liked to draw, Mama gave me a binder with lined notebook paper. Each afternoon I would watch a different monster movie and document it with crayon drawings. Frankenstein's Monster, the Wolfman, the Amazing Colossal Man, the Incredible Shrinking Man, the Blob, the Giant Gila Monster. My favorite movie had to be Abbott and Costello Meet Frankenstein, because you got three classic monsters in one movie (four if you counted Vincent Price's Invisible Man cameo at the end). Plus, Dracula and Wolfman were played by the original actors, Bela Lugosi and Lon Chaney Jr. I suppose my least favorite monster movie was The Monolith Monsters. What a rip-off! In my youthful mind, they were no more than oversized Magic Rocks.

Having been terminally bitten by the "monster bug", I began to expand my interest in monsters, the macabre, and horror in general as I grew older. First there were Aurora monster models at age eight through twelve. My mother, a horror enthusiast herself, kept my monster addiction well supplied. During our weekly visits to town, she would buy me a new monster model or a new issue of Famous Monsters of Filmland. I wanted to buy Creepy and Eerie, but Mama said they were much too 'adult' for me... especially the buxom Vampirella (which she considered to be the slutty, half-naked daughter of Satan himself). My mother also let me decorate my bedroom with posters of Count Dracula and King Kong. I did my very best to convince her that I would benefit greatly from a room painted entirely in black with a casket-shaped bed. She wasn't about to go quite that far, however, much to my disappointment.

Model building was a huge hobby of mine between the ages of ten and twelve. I built all the Aurora classic Universal movie monster models, which in the early 70s were the glow-in-the-dark models in the square box, not the older versions in the rectangular box. I never used the glow heads, hands, or feet, though. Even at that age, I was a stickler for detail, and so I painted the models as close to the cinematic monsters as I could (or I imagined them to be, since all of the Aurora models were from monster movies filmed in black and white.) I always saved the glow-in-the-dark pieces and built a "mini-monster" from the head, hands, and feet. There were other model series I built as well, like Planet of the Apes, Dark Shadows, Pirates of the Caribbean, Prehistoric Scenes, and Monster Scenes. The Monster Scenes models have become somewhat controversial over years for the fact that most of the sets involved torture, sadism, bondage, and sordid scientific experimentation. I never made that connection at age ten, but, looking back, the subject matter does seem questionable for young model-building boys who gleefully built pendulums and Iron Maidens to torment and terrify the scantly-clad female Victim. Joining ghoulish Dr. Deadly and the Frankenstein Monster was none other than sexy Vampirella in her nearly non-existent blood red outfit, showing off enough undead flesh to tempt and tantalize any prepubescent male. And, like the magazine, Mama refused to let me have the model version either, because I would actually be holding the nubile temptress in my sweaty little hand.

When I was twelve, I went into what I like to call my "Magic, Movies, and Ventriloquism" phase. I still loved my monsters, but my interests were focused on becoming an amateur magician and ventriloquist. I remember ordering magic tricks from the Johnson Smith Company and from the ad pages of comic books. When we made the sojourn to Disney World when I was twelve, I brought back some professional grade tricks from the now-defunct magic shop on the Magic Kingdom's Main Street. As for throwing my voice, I bought an instructional record by Edgar Bergan and learned his techniques. I had dummies of both Charlie McCarthy and Mortimer Snerd (I still have Mortimer, although he's a little worse for wear!).

I also developed an interest in movie projection. Daddy bought me a cheap projector from Sears one Christmas and I started collecting 8mm reels and watching some of my favorite monster movies, as well as old silent comedies starring Charlie Chaplin and Laurel and Hardy. True, they were only five minutes in length and were snippets of some of the more interesting scenes, in total silence. But there was a satisfying appeal to owning them on film, if only a small fragment. We could have never imagined back then that it would eventually become commonplace to own entire films, first on video tape, then on DVD and digital streaming.

I also borrowed an old 8mm movie camera from my aunt and started making my own movies. A lot of them were pretty bad and stupid, but I did experiment with stop motion a little, using clay figures that I sculpted myself. At that time, I was a huge fan of Ray Harryhausen and movies like *Jason and the Argonauts* and *The Seventh Voyage of Sinbad.* I also did a few crudely-orchestrated cartoons.

Of course, Halloween was always a huge holiday for me; one that I anticipated with the same reverence as Christmas. The month of October was always filled with planning Trick-or-Treating routes, the selection of just the right costume, and decorated the house, inside and out, for the big night.

But as I left childhood and approached my teenage years, I knew my indulgence in Halloween wouldn't last forever... that, as a faithful aficionado of All Hallows' Eve, my days were numbered.

Grits & Bits

Ego & Editing: You may believe your first draft is fine and dandy, that it requires a minimum of effort on your part in order to prepare it for submission to an editor or publisher. Don't deceive yourself. Ego and overconfidence can turn out to be two of your biggest obstacles. You will always be able to find things to be pruned and discarded in your prose; dusted off and spruced up with spit and polish. Edit, my fellow writers. Edit relentlessly, as though a pack of rabid dogs with English degrees were hot on your heels.

Character description: You don't always need to describe your characters down to the color socks they wear or that weird looking mole on the back of their neck. In short fiction, keep description minimal; the reader can usually fill in the blanks for themselves and conjure an image tailor-made for their individual imagination. With novel-length works, it's different. The characters will be on stage for several hundred pages and they deserve to be fleshed out more; physically and emotionally. The reader is making a major investment with longer pieces of fiction and you want them to feel as though the characters that are playing out the story are made of actual flesh and blood, not simply words. Paint a clear and distinct picture of them without overdoing it. When I first began writing, I had a bad habit of spending an entire page or two over-describing one particular character, probably to the point where the reader threw up their hands and said "Yeah, yeah, we know their eyes are a magical shade of hazel green with golden highlights that give them the luminescence of cat's eyes in the moonlight... but let's get on with the story, okay?" Now, I lay the character foundation just enough to allow a combination of the narrative of the story and the reader's imagination to do the rest. With experience and increased confidence, you'll come to the realization that less is definitely more

Writing the way you want to write: Not every writer can (or should) conjure the literary equivalent of filet mignon or lobster. Truth be told, my fiction is more akin to a Royal Crown Cola and a Moon pie... or gravy and biscuits. Nothing fancy... just fun and tasty fright food that sticks to your pulp-reading bones and fattens up your goosebumps every now and then.

Chapter Six

The Last Halloween

I n the little Tennessee town where I grew up, Halloween was for children. At the age of thirteen, you were pretty much expected to sit it out, hand out candy at the house with the old folks (your parents), or roll the principal's yard with two-ply Charmin. Now days, you can pretty much trick-or-treat until you're in your mid-twenties (freaky, but acceptable). Back in the late 60s and early 70s, you would be considered a "juvenile delinquent" if you showed up on someone's front porch with greasepainted face and one of your mother's spare pillowcases. The neighbors would be ready to call Joe Friday to come and haul you off to Juvie Hall.

My last real Halloween was in 1972... at least the last one that held all the privileges and benefits of childhood. As it drew near, I knew the end of something special was approaching and it saddened me. For as long as I could remember, Halloween had always been my favorite holiday. The smell of wood smoke in the air, the crunch of autumn leaves beneath the soles of your Red Ball sneakers, and the sense of adolescent community that the sight of dozens of Batmans (or is it *Batmen-*?), ballerinas, and Frankenstein's Monsters roaming from house to house brought. That and the gradually increasing heaviness of your candy sack taking on loot at each lighted porch or concrete stoop. Yes, it was downright magical... but those who held the Power... the *adults*... the mayor, the school superintendent, the local churches... said it all ended after the big One-Two. The pleasures of trick-or-treating were off limits for those acne-ridden, voice-changing, awkward creatures known as the common teenager.

I knew, for quite some time, that this had been coming. All good things – at least good *childhood* things – must come to an end. First Santa Claus, then the Easter Bunny, then your precious Mr. Potato Heads and G.I. Joes. I was a fighter, though. I wanted to cling to childhood with fingernails anchored to the quick and teeth bared... especially where All Hallows' Eve was concerned. So, I decided I would do the last one up right. Pull out all the stops. Gather up enough candy to last me at least until I was twenty.

My brother Kevin and my cousin Donna also sensed my impending doom. Their beloved Ronald, the Lover of Monsters (and Dum-Dums and Bite-Sized Snickers) was making a transition, albeit a forced one. At the beginning of October, we got together beneath the big magnolia tree in the back yard for a pow-wow.

"Won't you ever get to go trick-or-treating again?" Kevin asked me with a pout.

"No," I said grimly. "My time has come. Never again will I darken Old Lady Mangrum's door and hear her say 'Weren't you here an hour ago?' with her hair up in Coke can sized curlers and a Marlboro Light dangling from her lower lip.

"My confederates, ages eight and ten, still in their youthful prime, hung their heads in sorrow. Then we broke out the cherry Kool-Aid and Vanilla Wafers and partook of our final Halloween communion... and planned that season's festivities.

The following weekend we pooled our allowances and rode to town with our parents (for the entirety of our childhood, the city of Nashville was simply known as TOWN, at least to us rural rubes). We endured hair appointments and shoe shopping (a torture unto itself) and finally found ourselves in the hallowed halls of Grants Department Store. While our mothers went to the check the prices of cake pans and foundation bras ('unmentionables', to young ears), we loudly invaded the Halloween section of the store.

Grants was the best place to do one's Halloween shopping. The manager must surely have been a child at heart, because it was always decorated with plastic pumpkins, glow-in-the-dark skeletons, and cardboard cutouts of cackling witches and arch-backed black cats that looked as though they had stuck their claws in a light socket. The candy aisle with its three-pound bags of suckers, bubble gum, and candy bars was always fully stocked, enticing us with the sugary bootie to come. But the best thing about Grants' Halloween section was the costumes. For the little kids there were costumes in colorful cardboard boxes with clear windows with the masks of monsters, astronauts, and hollow-eyed princesses staring blankly through. Folded underneath those disembodied faces were silk-screened body stockings of shimmering polyester; the type that would make an Eskimo sweat and were, thank God, patently FLAME-RETARDANT!

We weren't interested in the baby stuff, though. We were interested in something else entirely. Grants had a large wooden bin that was perhaps six feet long by four feet wide... filled nearly two feet deep with rubber masks. Every sort of goblin or ghoul, werewolf or devil, could be found in that treasure trove of limp and garishly-painted latex. They were substandard in workmanship by today's standards, but back then they were wonderfully creepy works of art. With total abandon (and ignoring our mothers' forewarnings of "Don't you DARE try on those germy things!"), we picked through the heap of leering, grinning, fang-bearing rubber, trying on each and every one. Thinking back, I can still smell that powdery latex odor; feel the disorienting, but delicious, claustrophobia of staring through sagging eyeholes at the muted brilliance of Grants overhead fluorescent lights, and the sensation of the elastic string cutting into the back of my head. For a moment, you were transformed. No longer human but belonging to a time-honored fraternity of the grisly and ghoulish, hunted by torch-wielding mobs and cross-bearing Van Helsings in the mountainous wilds of Transylvania.

After the hunting was over, our choices were made. Mine was a pale-faced, widow-peaked vampire, fangs dripping with blood. My brother chose a leering, red-faced devil... then changed his mind and picked a werewolf when I convinced him that our conservative, Christian mom would never allow him to walk the length and breadth of Sunnyfield Drive bearing the unholy countenance of Satan. Cousin Donna opted for a different approach, shunning the latex and going with one of those bizarre transparent masks that showed a hint of your true face, while adding the benefit of bushy black eyebrows and mustache, or bee-stung lips the color of fire engine paint. She chose the Marilyn Monroe look and was certain that her mother would be more than happy to dye her hair platinum blond to complete the ensemble. Personally, I was doubtful that that would take place. My aunt Hazel was a bit more free-spirited than my mother, but I couldn't see her going down to the local Woolworths to buy a box of bleach-blonde Clairol to fulfill a ten-year-old's Halloween fantasy.

We left Grants satisfied, with masks and a couple of life-sized glow skeletons (if you can call five-foot-tall life-sized) in hand. The first step of the planning and execution of my Last Halloween had been completed. But there was work still to come.

Before I was a writer, I was known as an artist. Ever since I had scrawled my first Fred Flintstone and Touché Turtle on my stand-up blackboard at the age of four, family and friends honored me with distinction of being "the little boy who could draw".

It was no exception that October. I was on fire with artistic inspiration. Many a sheet of wide-ruled notebook paper fell victim to pencil-drawn renderings of the Wolfman, the Mummy, and my favorite, the Creature from the Black Lagoon, as well as assorted bats, rats, cats, and spiders. Perhaps I saw this as my last-ditch effort to purge myself of every Halloween image imaginable and share them with my friends. After all, that time the following year, I would see no jolly Jack-o-lanterns or grinning skeletons upon my classroom wall. Instead there would be boring charts of the food group pyramid, the American presidents (from Washington to Nixon), and the cryptic Table of Elements.

One drawing I was particularly fond of that year was a profile of a withered man with one bulging eye, a rat-gnawed ear, and a protruding chin sporting three ingrown hairs. The coupe-de-grace was a large ten-penny nail that had been driven through the bridge of his crooked nose. I was particularly proud of that addition. I could imagine that the Lunch Lady had put it there with a ball-peen hammer for the crime of not finishing his green bean casserole... or that he had done the piercing himself; a sideshow geek who had mutilated his Durante-sized schnoz for the enjoyment of the paying crowd.

That drawing was the most popular of my Halloween gallery and, before long, every boy and girl in my seventh-grade class was requesting a copy to hang on their front door for Halloween night. Being the congenial and agreeable lad that I was, I readily agreed... but it was a daunting task. There were no office copiers in that day and age, only primitive mimeograph machines with royal blue ink so toxic it would give a paper bag full of airplane model glue a solid run for its money. So, I set to work and hand-drew 32 of the one-eyed, nail-pierced geeks for my grinning classmates. Even the class bully wanted one. Inspired by his reign of terror, I added a word balloon hovering above the geek's snaggle-toothed mouth that pleaded "Here's my lunch money. Please don't hurt me!" The elementary school equivalent of Josepf Mengele thought this was absolutely hilarious and so I was spared a purple nurple or an Indian rope burn (of my choice) for the following week.

After school, I would go home and continue the planning of my final trick-or-treating campaign. Since I was going as Count Dracula, I wanted my outfit to be as authentic as possible. I had no flowing black cape – there was none to be bought back then, to my knowledge – but my father did have a long, navy blue overcoat that hung loosely and dangled past my knees (giving me sort of a Dark Shadows/Barnabas Collins look). I convinced my mother to let me wear my white Sunday shirt and necktie, but there would be no slacks or patent-leather shoes to complete the illusion of undeadness. This was a definite setback.

Who would ever believe the dreaded Nosferatu would terrorize the countryside wearing blue jeans from the boys department at Sears and ratty basketball high-tops?

Hours turned into days, days into weeks, and soon Halloween came to the picturesque town of Pegram (population 705). The weatherman had predicted rain, but our prayers apparently reached the Big Guy's celestial ears and the storm clouds held their bladders until well after nine o'clock. It was a chilly evening, blustery, sending dead leaves skittering across the streets like an exodus of withered, brown spiders. Kevin, Donna, and I donned our alter-egos and prepared for the "festival of groveling and begging", as my curmudgeonly Grandpa Kelly called it. We had our costumes satisfactorily in place (Donna with a fancy silk scarf wrapped around her head rather than the hair-sprayed helmet of platinum blonde tresses she had formerly envisioned).

Mama was in the kitchen, preparing her largest mixing bowl and filling it

with black and orange peanut butter kisses (the standard candy giveaway at the

Kelly household). She mugged a mock expression of terror as we paraded past in our garb. We had no plastic pumpkins or Halloween-themed bags to carry with us, so we went to the cabinet beneath the sink where Mama kept her spare grocery bags. We found three good-sized Kroger bags and, appropriating scissors, cut oval handles in the opposing sides. There were no 'Pubics' grocery stores (as Aunt Wanda calls them) during that day and time; only Kroger, A&P, and good old reliable Piggly-Wiggly.

"Y'all be careful," Mama called to us as we started for the front door. Daddy sat in the living room, listening to George Jones on the big console stereo. He threw up his hand and grinned. We waved back and headed into the

October night, the nasal tones of The Possum crooning "He Stopped Loving Her Today" drifting lazily behind us.

Now, you must understand; this was a different time. It was 1972. There was none of the fear of abductions and child molesters like there is today. Parents didn't follow their children around in cars and there was no such thing as trick-or-treating at the outlet mall or Trunk-or-Treat in the parking lot of the local church. Kids still had room to breathe and be kids, and one of the freedoms they enjoyed was venturing fearlessly into the night and trick-or-treating on their own.

I had secretly hoped for a full moon that evening – like any respectable vampire should – but if it was there, it was hidden behind a broad mat of dark clouds. We did our street first, going down one side, then back up the other. Although the temperature was hovering between the low 50s and high 60s, my rubber mask became sweltering. I began to sweat like a hog in a sauna and my frightening visage began to shift on me. I was leaving the McDowell house and heading across the yard, when the eyeholes of my vampire mask lost their alignment and, suddenly, I was as blind as a bat (no pun intended).

Suddenly, without warning, there was no ground beneath my feet. I took a spill and rolled into a drainage ditch. Fortunately, only my pride was hurt. I removed my mask and saw my brother and my cousin staring down at me.

"What are you doing in that ditch?" Kevin asked me.

"Remind me to pound you one when I get out!" I snapped.

There was one casualty to my fall in the ditch; my Kroger sack had split down the middle and the majority of the candy inside had scattered, like shrapnel from a detonated grenade. "Get your bottoms down in here and help me pick this stuff up," I told them (we didn't say 'ass' or even 'butt' back then; my mother said it was a 'vulgarity' and if she ever heard it cross our lips, we'd be walking the woods, picking our own switch).

Soon, we had the candy gathered and accounted for, bundled in the remains of the mangled bag. I couldn't help but moan when I saw that the next stop was Old Lady Mangrum's house. I slipped my mask back over my head, made sure the eyeholes were properly in place, and then we headed up the porch steps.

Old Lady Mangrum had no curlers in her hair that night, but the cigarette was there, as well as a suspicious look in her eyes. She examined my brother's costume closely. "Didn't I give you candy a half hour ago?" she asked. "I know I saw a dog like you come up here."

He was muffled, but I could hear the disdain in his voice. "I'm a werewolf."

When it was my turn, I held up my bag. "Do you have any Scotch tape?" I asked.

She told me to wait and then returned with a JC Penney shopping bag. It was big and roomy and would have held a bulldozer battery. "Thanks!" I said as I transferred my candy. Maybe my luck was turning for the better. This was, without a doubt, the Cadillac of Halloween bags.

We ended up trick-or-treating across the entire town of Pegram, which is no mean feat, since it is scarcely a half mile from entrance to exit. We had no watch to tell the time, but we knew it was getting late. My last Halloween was slowly winding down.

Before we headed home, we decided to visit one more place. It was pretty ordinary; a ranch-style house with white brick and a big picture window in the front. There was a Jack-o-lantern on the porch and black and orange crepe paper draped from the banisters. Thinking it was a safe bet, we mounted the porch and knocked on the door.

A lady appeared; tall, skinny, with a beehive hairdo that had gone out of style with the Johnson Administration. She seemed excited to see us. "Come in, come in!" she urged. "I have something to show you!" Her enthusiasm was a little disturbing, but we went in anyway. I don't know why, but we did.

The living room was dimly lit and there were candles everywhere; on the end tables, the fireplace mantle, on the bar counter of the kitchenette nearby. "Come here!" the woman beckoned with a bony finger. "He wants to talk to you!"

Suddenly, a creepy feeling ran down my spine. *He? Who is he?*

Then we stepped further into the living room and we knew. It was a man – a pretty overweight man, perhaps 300 pounds or more – sitting in a reclining chair, dressed in a wife-beater undershirt, flannel pajama pants, and bedroom slippers. But that wasn't the odd thing about him. His pudgy face was painted up like a clown and he wore a huge multi-colored wig on top of his head. He smiled lopsidedly at us and waved his hand. "Come here, kids!" he said, laughing sinisterly. "Come here... I have something to give you!"

Cautiously, we crept forward. We were scarcely four feet from the chair when I smelled the odor of beer and perspiration in the air. I saw a Budweiser can on an end table beside him. Looking around, I saw that there were several more sitting on the carpet beside his Lazy-Boy recliner.

"Open your bags!" he urged, still laughing. "Open 'em up and I'll give it to you!"

My brother stared at me with frightened eyes. I'd never seen a lycanthrope look so scared before.

Then the drunken guy in the clown makeup and the rainbow afro dropped foil-wrapped popcorn balls in our treat bags and said, "Happy Halloween!"

A few minutes later, we were outside and back on the street. We looked at each other and began to giggle... but there was more relief to our mirth than humor.

"That was so *weird*!" Donna said.

"You've got that right," I said. My heart was still pounding in my chest.

"What are we going to do with *these*?" Kevin asked, holding the crazy clown's popcorn ball in his hand.

We looked at one another, then tossed them in the nearest ditch and started home.

Halfway there, my brother turned to me. "So... you're not going trick-or-treating with us next year?"

"I can't dress up," I told him, "but I can walk with you."

He nodded quietly, then rummaged through his bag for a Bit-O-Honey.

Thinking back, I'm not sure if I ever did. The last Halloween I remember as a child, was the one we shared together in the fall of 1972.

These days I have three kids of my own. One has outgrown the joys and thrills of Halloween (having traded it in for a boyfriend, an iPhone, and an Xbox), while two still indulge in the same autumnal rituals I enjoyed as a child.

Things have changed now. Small town Halloweens are similar to the ones I enjoyed, but they have an edge to them now; a constant awareness that things are not always right in our world. I'm always a few steps behind them, making sure they don't step off the edge of a sidewalk, or that they don't stray too close to a patch of darkness between trees or shrubs. I reckon a parent has a right to be overly cautious in this day and time. There are dangers out there; dangers that were probably there when I was a kid, but not quite so apparent and identifiable.

But they have fun and, through the eyes of their masks and their infectious laughter, I relive the spirit of Halloweens past. Not as carefree and innocent as I once had it, but fun, nonetheless.

And if we end up with popcorn balls given away by demented clowns, we simply toss them in the nearest ditch and go our merry way.

Grits & Bits

Simplifying Dialogue: A long time ago, when I was a green, wet-behind-the-ears writer, Joe Lansdale shared a bit of advice with me. "When it comes to writing dialogue, it's better to just say 'said'." At a time where I had my characters 'exclaiming', 'explicating', and 'ejaculating' everything they said (just imagine what kind of image that last one puts in your reader's mind!), Joe's advice took away the pressure of needing to sound 'literary'. I found using "asked" instead of "inquired", and "said" instead of "explained" and "expounded", worked just as well, especially in my own brand of rural fiction. Simplification of dialogue can help the narrative flow easier and bring the reader through the story faster, without laboring over trying to decipher how or why a character is actually "saying" something.

Handling Rejection: No one likes rejection, but if you want to make it as a published writer, you're bound to get your share of rejection slips. Just because a story or novel you write, maybe even spent months or years rewriting, editing, and polishing, isn't accepted, doesn't mean that it is a piece of crap. Editors and publishers reject submissions for many reasons. Maybe they have reached their set limit of how many stories they can accept for a particular anthology or issue of a magazine. Or perhaps it just doesn't suit their needs at the present time. If that's the case, straighten that backbone and submit to someone else. Impatience is common, especially when you have attempted to break into your chosen genre and have struck out, time after time, for a lengthy period of time. Heck, it took me twelve long years of submitting to a steady stream of markets to finally make my first sale. And there were some magazines, like the late David Silva's *The Horror Show*, that I never could sell anything too, despite the fact that I submitted to it fifty or more times.

And don't let your ego get in the way and cause you to do something stupid. It is immature and completely unprofessional for anyone to bad-mouth or give a publisher grief over something so minor and commonplace as a rejection. My advice to the disgruntled submitter: treat potential publishers with the calm courtesy and professionalism that you would expect from them. If not, word will spread quickly and your reputation as a whiner and troublemaker will get you absolutely nowhere.

Chapter Seven

Pow, Zap, Ka-Boom!

The Comic Book Years

C omic books were always a peripheral interest for me when I was a kid. I was five years old when Adam West and Burt Ward donned the cowl and little, black mask and tooled around Gotham City in that ultra-cool 1955 Lincoln Futura turned Batmobile (still the best cinematic representation, in my opinion). I loved that campy show and its colorful gallery of rouges passionately and was parked in front of the black and white Zenith twice a week in breathless anticipation, same Bat Time, same Bat Channel. I did watch reruns of the old black and white Superman series with George Reeves, but other than that, my awareness of superheroes was limited. I was still heavily invested in monsters and caped crime fighters were fun, but merely a pleasant diversion and nothing more.

I don't remember actually reading comic books until I was eight or nine, and it was an irregular occurrence.

Mama would buy me one after a doctor or dentist visit, or Daddy would buy me a stack to take on daytrips to places like Rock City in Chattanooga, Beech Bend Park in Bowling Green, or the Memphis Zoo (the only three vacation destinations I remember until we started traveling to Florida in my early teens). My favorites were always *Batman* (of course) and *The Flash*, and I remember buying *Justice League* and *Teen Titans* every now and then. I was strictly a DC fan back then and really had no awareness of Marvel at that point. I also read a lot of *Richie Rich, Classics Illustrated,* and *Sad Sack* (which my father loved because it reminded him of his Army days). I may have bought *The Incredible Hulk* once or twice, but mainly because he reminded me of a rampaging Frankenstein's Monster in bright purple britches.

It wasn't until I was fifteen or sixteen that I really became enamored with comics and comic book collecting. My knowledge of superheroes almost became encyclopedic in nature at that point and the discovery of the Marvel Comic Universe was like unearthing the legendary Holy Grail. *Batman* was still a huge favorite, but *The Amazing Spiderman, The Incredible Hulk, The Fantastic Four,* and *Captain America & The Falcon* followed on the Caped Crusader's heels, as well as *The Uncanny X-Men* (especially when the international line-up began in 1975's *Giant-Size X Men*, starring Wolverine, Nightcrawler, Storm, Colossus, and others). I was also heavily into the horror comics; *House of Mystery, House of Secrets, the Unexpected, Swamp Thing, Werewolf by Night, Tomb of Dracula, Man Thing,* and *Ghost Rider.* And I began collecting reprints of the old EC Horror comics as well; titles like *Tales from the Crypt, Haunt of Fear,* and *Vault of Horror.*

Naturally, being the amateur artist that I was, I began to draw superheroes more and more. I still loved my monsters, but I'm afraid they took a backseat to costumed crime fighters during my freshman and sophomore years of high school. My knowledge of human anatomy sharpened as I learned to draw heroic musculature in motion and my first involvement with plot and visual storytelling took place as I began to construct crude comic books of my own. These always starred DC or Marvel heroes, because at that point I had no idea that characters were copyrighted properties. Of course, there was little chance that either of the big comic conglomerates were going to notice a geeky country boy's maladjusted scribblings and send a legal goon squad to the speck-on-the-map town of Pegram, Tennessee to threaten me to cease and desist.

My interest in comic book collecting and creating ramped up a hundredfold during my junior year in high school in 1975. A classmate in Drivers Ed, Lindsey Cunningham, noticed my interest in drawing comics and said "You ought to hang out with my brother, Lowell. He's *really* into that kind of stuff."

Now, I knew that I had Lowell in some of my other classes, but we had never formally met. From first impressions, he seemed stoic and no nonsense, highly intelligent with a dry sense of humor; sort of a teenaged Sherlock Holmes in nature. Lindsey introduced us and a nerdy friendship was born. Our mutual interest in comics forged a creative alliance and we began to produce our own comic books. Lowell did the writing and I did the drawing. We weren't exactly Stan Lee and Jack Kirby, but we did okay for two teenage boys with aspirations of making it big in the comic book business someday. We ended up collaborating on a couple of characters Lowell had created. One was KA, Son of RA, an eagle-headed superhero based on the deity in Egyptian mythology. The other was a silver-haired, covert operative with ninja skills and a steel bow staff named Wolf.

After several collaborations, I was inspired to write and create my own characters and stories (it wasn't a creative breakup of the magnitude of the Beatles, or even a breakup at all, just a natural progression that Lowell seemed perfectly okay with). Before long, I had my own stable of comic book heroes to draw upon; the violent, revenge-obsessed Adversary, the frog-headed Amphibi-Human (a science experiment gone horribly wrong, like in the old Vincent Price movie, The Fly), the laser-shooting, unbreakable Glassman, and a mysterious, mute motorcycle-riding crusader known as the Rebel. I was a huge reader of Bantam Books' paperback reprints of the *Doc Savage* pulp series at that time, as well as *The Avenger* and *The Shadow-*, so I ended up creating my own pulp character, the Piranha, a Navy Seal type hero of the 1930s who turned to crime-fighting and mob-busting, with the help of a team of quirky, but helpful aides (what pulp hero of that era didn't have their band of scientific experts and brothers-in-arms?). I had also developed an interest in reading traditional western novels around that time; rip-roaring fiction by Louis L'Amour, Zane Grey, and Charles Portis, as well as a particularly violent series called *Edge* by George G. Gilman. So, I came up with my own western character named Dead-Eye; a former Confederate soldier turned gunfighter after he returns home to find his family murdered by a band of outlaws.

I drew several issues of each character's comic, except Dead-Eye, which, in my mind, was more suited to the written word than a graphic depiction. The superhero comics became quite popular around the school, even with many of the teachers. A few were in full color, but most were in black and white with pencil shading on white copy paper, bound in notebooks (which, thankfully, I still have in my possession). At the time, I was also the cartoonist for the school newspaper, *Cub Scripts*, and had a regular comic strip called Pimples McCrab. Pimples was a devious, ne'er-do-well high schooler, whose pranks and schemes always backfired on him.

It was around the beginning of my senior year – probably the fall of 1976 – that I got the hare-brained idea to actually take my comic book artist aspirations a step further... a big, clumsy, overly-ambitious step, to put it lightly. I actually sent some of my drawings and story ideas to one of the big two. I sent the Amphibi-Human to DC Comics.

Even with such dumb-ass kid bravado, I still figured it wouldn't pan out to anything and that I would either find the return envelope in my mailbox in a week or two, with the contents utterly ignored, or that I would hear nothing at all. But, as it turned out, that wasn't the case. I received a very nice and informative letter from someone on the DC editorial staff ... someone by the name of Jack. I wasn't sure if he was a regular editor there or simply an art editor, but he seemed to be genuinely interested in my aspirations in becoming a comic book artist. A strange sort of friendship was formed in the months afterward between that New York City editor and this shy, introverted high school student in the Tennessee sticks. He gave me pointers about comic layout, not crowding your panels, dialogue, story progression... stuff like that. And we went back and forth some about Amphibi-Human, too. Sure, it was probably a dumb idea – a superhero with a giant frog head, arm, and leg – but he said it had the same dark, bayou feel as Swamp Thing and he didn't seem to treat it as some big joke. We even batted a couple of plausible premises concerning AH back and forth, but none of them turned into anything concrete. This correspondence, a total of eight letters in all, eventually petered out and ended. I don't remember it disappointing me; even at that young age (I graduated when I was seventeen, so I was no more than sixteen at the time), I knew that Jack was a busy man and probably didn't have time to waste on some teenager who had dreams of being a comic book artist. But he had taken the time and I was grateful for that. One of the bits of wisdom he had imparted in one of his final letters was that it was very unlikely that I would be able to make it as a bonafide comic artist unless I was based in or near the Big Apple. Even as naive as I was, I knew this was true. And it was around that time that the writing portion of my creative interests began to outweigh the need to render my thoughts visually. So, I stuck those DC letters into a notebook on my bedroom shelf and forgot all about them.

Funny thing about sticking stuff away like that. Years – maybe even decades – later they have a strange way of turning back up. A few years ago, I was going through some old papers and, lo and behold, there they were... the letters. I opened up the first one I had received, a rather long but encouraging one, complimenting me on my desire to draw and create comics. In the left border was the big DC emblem with all the big heroes standing one atop the other's shoulders – Superman, Batman, Wonder Woman, the Flash, Green Lantern, and so on. At the bottom, the editor had scrawled his full name. In all the correspondence afterward, he had simply signed it "Jack".

Something about the way that signature looked bugged me a little. It seemed downright *familiar*. I still had some reprints of the old EC Horror comics and I found one bearing my favorite cover. Tales of the Crypt, Number 39. A knife-wielding maniac chasing three young boys through a graveyard. In a small circle at one of the terrified kid's right elbow was the artist's classic signature. It looked identical to the signature at the bottom of that letter.

Hell, no, I told myself. *It couldn't have been.* And then I put that letter, and the others, away and left it at that.

But that question stuck in the back of my brain like a thorn and never went away. And just recently, maybe no more than a couple of months ago, I asked someone about the possibility of that DC staff member being who I suspected him to be. Someone who had quite a bit of knowledge of comic book history and who had actually worked for both DC and Marvel from time to time.

So, I texted horror author Brian Keene and asked him.

ME: "Could you see if you could find an answer to a question for me, hoss? Did EC Comics/Mad Magazine artist Jack Davis ever work as an art director/editor at DC? When I was trying to make it as a comic book artist back in 1976, I had a long-running correspondence with a Jack Davis there. The signatures on the letters I still have resemble his classic signature. I was wondering if he could have been one and the same."

The answer came almost immediately.

BRIAN: "Yes indeed! That's pretty awesome!"

Afterward, I posed this question to a couple of others... and they gave me the same affirmative answer. But, I've also had others balk and dispute the notion. "Jack Davis was one of the biggest cartoonists and illustrators of the 1970's. He did work for Mad Magazine, TV Guide, magazine advertisements... he couldn't have worked for DC, too!" True, he did all that. But he was a very busy and versatile man and maybe he took a steady job, between all that freelance work. And, from everything I've read, he was just the kind of guy that might have taken time to encourage a young artist with dreams of comic book grandeur. Jack Davis died in 2016, so I may never know 100% if it was actually him. But I like to think it was... and that I experienced a brush with greatness at an early age and didn't even know it.

Oh, and one more thing before we leave the subject of comic books and move onward. A few years after graduating high school, around 1989, my old classmate Lowell Cunningham called me at home with some good news. He had sold a comic book series to Aircel Comics (later Malibu). It was about an international - intelligence organization that investigated paranormal and extraterrestrial activity on Earth. The agents wore dark suits and sunglasses. I wished him well with the series and told him I'd track down a copy of the first issue at my local comics store (at that time The Great Escape in nearby Nashville). But my love and fascination with comic books had pretty much faded by then, and I forgot the name of Lowell's comic series and never did seek it out.

Then, in 1997, I went to see *Men in Black* in the theater. It was already a week or so into its run and was a huge success. Imagine my shock and surprise when the opening credits rolled and "Based on the Malibu comic by Lowell Cunningham" flashed before my eyes.

I sat there dumbfounded. *So that's what he was talking about!* I thought to myself.

So, two teenage boys started out with dreams of comic book stardom in a rural, Tennessee high school. One had realized his dream, saw it in publication, and then depicted – numerous times – on the silver screen.

The other had taken a different path; one paved with the written word rather than brightly colored comic panels. And, as it turned out, it would be a particularly long one, full of hard work, doubt, and rejection, before success finally came.

My Ten Favorite Movies (Horror)

1. Creature From the Black Lagoon
2. The Haunting (1963)
3. The Thing (1982)
4. Let's Scare Jessica to Death (1971)
5. The Legend of Hell House (1972)
6. Halloween III: Season of the Witch (1982)
7. Jaws (1975)
8. Psycho (1960)
9. Alien (1979)
10. Dark Night of the Scarecrow (1981)

Chapter Eight

The Writing Bug

A round the end of my sixteenth year, I got bit by the Writing Bug.

For me, it just seemed to be a natural progression from comic book artist to comic book artist/writer to simply 'writer'. I still did some comic books on the side, but since I was aware that I would pretty much have to leave Tennessee and move north to New York to make my mark in comics, I decided to focus on purely writing fiction. Little did I know, that writing short stories and novels is a whole lot different than writing caption boxes and filling word balloons with snappy dialogue.

Reading had much to do with my desire to write. Since the 8th grade I had been a voracious reader. It started with nonfiction books and biographies of historical figures, checked out of the little library at Pegram Elementary ("He has read 86 books in one year!" my teacher, Miss Carrie Street proclaimed proudly to my mother at a parents/teacher conference). Then I gravitated to the classics, but those dealing with the macabre and science fiction. I had gone to a book fair at Cheatham County High in my freshman year and purchased two books. One was Bram Stoker's *Dracula* and the other an anthology of horror and suspense stories called *Alfred Hitchcock Presents: Stories to be Read With the Door Locked.* The latter boasted a lot of great stories, including one in particular that chilled me to the bone. Waldo Carlton Wright's *Little Foxes Sleep Warm*, a tale about a farmer suffering through hard times who freezes his wife until spring thaw to save her from starvation (and the horrifying payoff in the ending paragraph) showed me that short fiction could be told effectively and with maximum impact in a minimal amount of words (a mere nine pages.)

More classics of horror and fantasy followed. *The Strange Case of Doctor Jekyll & Mister Hyde* by Robert Louis Stevenson, *The Invisible Man, War of the Worlds,* and *Food of the Gods* by H.G. Wells, *Journey to the Center of the Earth* and *20,000 Leagues Under the Sea* by Jules Verne, and about anything written by Ray Bradbury, Edgar Allen Poe, and Ambrose Bierce. I tried desperately to digest H.P. Lovecraft's Cthulhu mythos stories, but at age fourteen it was a losing battle. Lovecraft's prose and concepts completely went over my head, although a few like "Rats in the Walls" and "Cool Air" were more down to earth and relatable.

I also read a ton of the Bantam, Pyramid, and Warner paperbacks of pulp heroes like Doc Savage, The Shadow, and The Avenger. Around age fifteen, I was never without a Doc Savage in hand, even on day trips with the family or vacations to Florida. I also started reading westerns, mostly Louis L'Amour and a particularly violent western series by George Gillman called *Edge.* These were all quick reads – 150 pages or less – and fueled my nearly insatiable hunger for adventure and escapism. I also read the true crime book *Helter Skelter* by Vincent Bugliosi in 1976, the same time that the CBS mini-series starring Steve Railsback was aired. I remember it being quite a bit stronger in content and much more graphic than what was depicted on television. The killing and mutilation of Sharon Tate and her friends was described in great detail and there were grisly facts that were only mentioned in the book (like Manson's plan to cut out Elizabeth Taylor's eyes and hack off Richard Burton's penis and preserve them in a jar of alcohol together.)

One book that was a major catalyst in generating the desire to write within me was Harper Lee's *To Kill a Mockingbird.* I had watched the movie several times on television and loved it, but I had never read the actual book. Harper's book captivated me in a different way that the film did. The Southern settings, down home dialogue, and the strong anti-racism theme engaged me on entirely different level. Plus, there were several scenes in the book that weren't portrayed in the film, which made the narrative more poignant. After reading the last page of *Mockingbird,* I knew, without a doubt, what I wanted to do with my life. I wanted to be a writer.

I took three key classes in my senior year of high school. One was Mrs. Hart's Creative Writing class, the second was Miss Cooper's Journalism, and the third was Modern History with Mr. Darrow. Each one was instrumental in adding fuel to the fire as far as my desire to write was concerned.

Creative Writing gave me the freedom to simply sit down and experiment; cut my teeth on creating with prose rather than artistic images. It was a liberating experience. Before then, I considered myself solely an artist who wanted to create stories revolving around my art. Now, the art was secondary and the written word was the most important aspect of my creative process. Mrs. Hart pretty much let us do the sort of writing we felt motivated to do. Sure, we had assignments: haiku, traditional poetry, short fiction, etc., but she gave us the leeway to write what interested us most. I forged a friendship with two fellow classmates – Scott Magill and Donald Belcher – and we seemed to thrive on creating stories and reading each other's work (and, I must admit, indulge in a generous amount of horseplay in the process). We even collaborated on a comic book called *The Destroyers*, about a trio of military soldiers who teleport themselves into prehistoric times to battle dinosaurs and cavemen (I know, chronologically impossible... but we were budding writers, not science majors).

Miss Cooper's Journalism class was more structured and serious. Since the school paper, *Cub Scripts*, was an extension of the journalism class, assignments sometimes added content to the monthly periodical. In addition to continuing my Pimples McCrab comic strip, I also wrote news articles and commentaries. We also did debates in Journalism, debating for or against certain topics with fellow students, then shifting gears and debating for the opposite side. This taught me a lot about objectivity and seeing the world through other folks' eyes, as well as realizing that things aren't always set in stone... that there are pros and cons, and value in listening to and understanding opposing viewpoints, in all subjects and situations.

Mr. Darrow's Modern History class was a pure pleasure, especially for a history buff such as myself. I had developed into an avid Civil War and Old West aficionado by then and Darrow's class was right down my alley. He was never hesitant about supplying us with seamy historical facts and statistics ("75% of men in the Old West suffered from one form of venereal disease or another due to the amount of 'soiled doves' that made their living throughout the cattle and mining towns.") or his own personal opinions on various historical heroes ("The Earp brothers were no more than western gangsters, using their badges and law enforcement credentials to gain the gambling monopoly in Tombstone, of which Ike Clanton and his followers were their direct competition. That eventually led to tension between the two factions, culminating in the infamous Gunfight at the O.K. Corral.")

We had no textbooks in Modern History. Mr. Darrow would simply lecture about the West or World War II or the Russian Revolution, and we would sit there and absorb it all. For tests, he would tell us to write down everything we remembered about that particular subject. And this history teacher had been so engaging and entertaining that I had no trouble at all writing, almost word for word, everything that he had said. It was that class that increased my interest in American history, especially the periods between 1861 and 1950, and prompted me to explore those eras in my own fiction later on.

One of my major influences during those high school years (and for years afterward, until her death at the age of ninety-eight in 1990) was definitely my maternal grandmother. Grandmama Spicer was a master storyteller; a vocal conveyor of family history, ghost lore, and tall tales. I had grown up listening to her stories peripherally; while my cousins and I played around the front porch in the summer or on short road trips to Rock City in Chattanooga or Beech Bend Park in Bowling Green. It wasn't until my teenage years when I really began to sit down and listen. And I did listen, for hours at a time. Like Mr. Darrow, Grandmama had a way of telling a tale that stuck with you. She had a down-home, folksy style of spinning a yarn or relating things of the past that was like water to a sponge. And there were weird and horrifying tales she told that appealed to my own love of the bizarre and unusual; tales that I still recall, word for word, today. The story about her and her childhood friend walking along a stone wall near an abandoned house and how that friend fell into a thorny garden of Devil's Ear cactuses, and died a few days later when the quills worked their way through her body and skewered her heart. Or the battalion of headless Confederate calvary horsemen who haunted a country road, as well as the ghostly sounds of a stick of firewood hitting flesh in an abandoned house, where a man had murdered his wife decades before she was born. Years later, when I actually began to submit horror fiction for publication, I would draw on some of Grandmama's front porch stories for inspiration, adapting them in prose, in my own voice and style, but still with her unmistakable storytelling ability as my guide.

During that last year of high school, I wrote several short stories. All were crudely structured and orchestrated, but showed promise and imagination, according to Mrs. Hart. One was about an escaped convict who was hiding from bloodhounds in a crawlspace beneath an abandoned house and got bit by dozens of blue-tailed skinks (a lizard down here in the South) which paralyzed him (end of story). The other was about a child abuser set upon by a shadowy group of vigilantes dressed in black (all formerly abused children themselves) and fatally dealt justice in with angry fists, as they mourned the child who had been beaten by the perpetrator moments before. These tales were far from perfect, but at least I was making an effort. Mrs. Hart suggested I submit the child abuse story to *Cub Scripts*, but, self-consciously, I never did.

I also wrote my first novel that year; a short one to be sure, perhaps fifteen chapters in length. It was a Dystopian drama titled *Beyond the Walls*, in which New York City has become so violent and crime-ridden that huge concrete walls have been erected around the borders of Manhattan Island, cutting it off from the outside world. A group of five teenagers with various weapons (that seemed to be a theme with me during those early days) uncover a government conspiracy and plot to escape the island to freedom. I actually found an agent in the classifieds of an issue of *Writer's Digest* and mailed it to them for consideration. They turned it down, saying that they were no longer taking submissions. At the time, I believed them. After coming across it in my files a few months ago, I figured it was just a polite way of saying it was a crudely plotted and totally unsaleable piece of crap (which I really have no argument with). Incidentally, years later, I went to see John Carpenter's *Escape from New York* and became convinced that the *Halloween* director had come across my idea somewhere and stole it. Of course, that was ridiculous, but when you are an Angry Young Man and struggling to publish after years of constant failure, you tend to have those types of delusions (we'll get to my Angry Man phase in a later chapter, I promise you.)

So, there I was at the latter half of my senior year. 1977, on the verge of graduation and believing I was destined to be the next Stephen King (doesn't all wanna-be horror writers at the age of seventeen?). I was continuing with my writing, both in Creative Writing and at home. Up until that point, I had been writing in longhand, on regular school paper or a legal pad. But I craved to write 'professionally' on a typewriter. I expressed my wants to my parents, and one evening Daddy brought home an ancient black 1920 Underwood Number 5. It was the kind you see in the newspaper offices in those old black and white noir movies. Big and clunky and fifty pounds if it was an ounce. I loved the sound – that clackity-clack-clack-ding! – but it wasn't as easy as I expected. I had to teach myself to type using a self-teaching book and when you made mistakes, it was glaringly obvious. But I limped along with that old relic, hoping that something better might come along soon.

A few weeks before graduation, I mentioned to one of my teachers that I wouldn't be going to college. Now, you had to know my family dynamics to understand this. I came from farmers and blue collar workers, and not one of them or their offspring had ever achieved higher education past the 12th grade. You were expected to throw that flat-topped graduation cap up in the air, take a couple of weeks off, and then go to work. I'd already talked it over with Mama and Daddy, and they agreed that I could take a year to try my hand at writing and attempting to get published. But I knew, eventually, if the writing didn't take right off, I'd be wearing steel-toed boots and punching a time-clock somewhere.

Anyway, I mentioned my plans (or lack of plans) to that teacher and she got this shocked, sorrowful look on her face... as though she had gotten news that someone had kicked the bucket. "Oh... I'm so sorry to hear that." She placed a sympathetic hand on my shoulder and looked like she was about to cry. "I'm afraid you'll never be a published writer if you don't attend college."

Maybe she thought that awful revelation would make me as sad as she was at that moment. But all it did was make me mad. *How dare she think that I don't have the God-given talent to make it in the writing business!* I thought to myself. *Why, I'll be handing her my first published novel in a year's time. Then she'll eat her words!* (That's how naive, full-of-it seventeen-year-olds react when a teacher – no, a freaking *mentor* – seemingly sets out to squash your hopes and dreams.)

Graduation day came. We walked the line, accepted our diplomas, threw our hats in the air, said goodbye and left. For graduation presents, I got fifty bucks and a set of weights from Mama and Daddy, and other gifts (including that cherished five dollar bill from Grandpa Kelly). Then I set to work writing.

I wrote and I wrote... and I wrote some more. I bought the big hardcover Writer's Digest directory with all the addresses of paying markets and agents ready to tuck your book beneath their arm and run it to the nearest big-name publisher. And I bought a big hardcover Roget's Thesaurus, too... because, you know, you can't use the same word too many times before folks start thinking you're stuck in neutral. If you can say it fifty-two different ways, it's better. Right?

Then with a folder full of ammunition, I began to submit. I began to stuff those manila envelopes and lick postage stamps. But no dice. Submission after submission came back with the same old note. "Thank you, but your submission fails to meet our needs at this time." Some didn't come back at all, as if the mailman had hand-delivered it to some black hole or portal to another dimension. As my free year of writing began to dwindle and Daddy kept giving me that *look* and asking me from time to time what my shoe size was, I began to get the sinking feeling that this writing dream wouldn't come as easily as I had imagined it would.

As seventeen slipped away and I turned eighteen ('a real man's working age', my father imparted with stern wisdom), I knew that best-selling lists and book signings with mile-long waiting lines wouldn't be coming anytime soon.

It was 1978 and I was a young man.

But I wasn't a happy one.

Grits & Bits

Traveling the middle ground: When you're a writer, you have choices... many choices. First or third person narrative? What plot to explore? What place in time will the particular piece of fiction take place, the cast of characters, etc., etc. Then there is the selection of fiction length to consider. Does this particular idea merit the bumper-car or Scrambler version of a short story? Or does the mother of all roller coasters – the full-length novel – suit your needs? Sometimes the choice comes easy... sometimes it takes a little soul-searching and consideration to make up your mind.

And sometimes you have no choice but to travel the middle ground. That means penning a long fiction piece: a novelette or a novella. Unlike short stories, which normally run between 1,500 and 7,500 words, or novels, which stretch between 40,000 and 120,000 words (or even more), the novelette runs the gamut between 7,500 and 17,500 words and the novella between 17,500 and 40,000 words. Sometimes an idea warrants a longer treatment than a short story and a shorter one than a novel. Thus, rather than a vignette or an epic journey, you set out to write a substantial adventure through the particular genre you happen to specialize in. I, of course, prefer the kind with spooks and spiders and things that go bump (and bite) in the night.

Conquering distraction during the writing process: You know what I'm talking about. You sit down at the keyboard, sincerely intent on getting some serious writing done, feeling good about the idea in your head and the wonderful prose that is just aching to spring from your fingertips, through the keys, and onto the monitor. Then your phone dings. A text from a family member or friend. Heaven forbid you be rude and refrain from answering it! So, you do and a full-blown conversation takes place. Or you see a notification pop up concerning Twitter or Facebook, and you know you've got to check it out and see what all the fuss is about. Usually it is something controversial and inflammatory, so you simply have to read every single comment. Or it could be one of your young'uns, wanting a snack or excitedly acting out an episode of Peppa Pig or Paw Patrol in lavish detail. And then there's the dog, also begging for a snack or a trip outside for a pee break, or the cat wanting a lap snuggle or hopping up to tap-dance maliciously across your keyboard. And let's not even mention the overwhelming urge to binge watch that new show on Netflix, Hulu, or Disney+.

There are ways to avoid such distracting pitfalls. You can lock yourself away in your private writing area (man-cave, she-shed, or the guest bedroom no potential guest has ever slept a night in) with a DO NOT DISTURB! sign dangling from the knob... and be sure to draw a menacing little skull-and-crossbones for emphasis. Some writers actually wear earplugs or sound-deafening muffs to give them complete silence. Others actually *want* sound to shut the other distractions out. I personally know a lot of writers who listen to music while they write. I, myself, like to write listening to various types of music, according to what sort of fiction I'm involved in at the time: bluegrass, country, and Southern rock like Lynyrd Skynyrd and ZZ Top for my dark rural tales, heavy metal such as Metallica, Judas Priest, and Ozzy for extreme horror, and when I'm writing western horror like my Dead-Eye series, Ghoultown and the spaghetti western themes of Ennio Morricone.

If you have a noisy and chaotic family life (the way I did until the kids became teens and became hermits in their own rooms), you simply learn to tune everything else out. A small nuclear device or a tornado could wreck the house and you will still be in your 'zone', typing away, oblivious to the pandemonium around you.

Chapter Nine

Angry Young Man

E very writer walks through the fire. A period of trial and error, frustration and doubt. Countless rejection slips and lack of positive response from editors and publishers. Wondering if you are cut out to be a writer, whether you have the talent and ability to make it, fearing that you are just spinning your wheels for no good reason at all.

My period spanned twelve years; from 1976 to 1988.

I went to work in the summer of 1978, sweating and straining and busting my ass in a grocery distribution warehouse in the industrial district of Nashville. My uncle, James, had worked there before and said it was an easy job. The fact was, he had worked in the 'tobacco room', kept cool with air conditioning, pulling orders of cigarettes, chewing tobacco, and cigars. I, however, ended up working in the main warehouse, from seven at night to seven the next morning, three and a half nights a week. No air conditioning whatsoever and hotter than hell. A train ran through the middle of the warehouse and, except for the entrance and exit for the train and the bay doors on the dock, there were no windows in the place. You didn't know whether it was night or day at any given hour.

My first day, I felt like Daniel thrown into the lion's den. The workers mainly consisted of ex-cons, drug addicts, alcoholics, and mentally unbalanced folks. And here I was, the direct opposite of them all; young, unexperienced, naïve. I soon discovered that it could be a dangerous place. A couple of the guys took me under their wing, taught me what to do to fit in, where to go and not go in the big, shadowy warehouse. I later discovered that some of the workers wandered off to places during their breaks to shoot up, gamble, or sneak prostitutes in for sex. And that if you happened upon the wrong person at the wrong time, you could end up getting hurt very badly or even raped, if they had that inclination. It had happened there before. It could happen again just as easily, if an unseasoned young man like myself found himself suddenly among the wrong company.

During the three months I worked there, I discovered that the ugly old ways of the South still existed and that racism still flourished in such places. There were two restrooms with the breakroom and vending machines in between them. I kept going to the restroom on the left because it was cleaner than the other one. On my third night there, one of the workers pulled me aside.

"What're you doing going in *their* bathroom?" he asked. "The black bathroom."

Like back in the fifties and sixties, the bathroom facilities in the warehouse was segregated. Whites went in one and blacks in the other. It was the same with the two water fountains. It was confusing and made me uneasy. After elementary school, high school had seemed to been an even playing field; students of various races getting along with very little evidence of prejudice. Then the first job I get and it's back to distrust and suspicion; take a crap in your bathroom, but stay the hell out of mine.

After leaving that place, I went on to other jobs. Custodian, shipping receiving clerk, assistant drugstore manager. Most of these were on third shift. I would work all night, come home and write half a day, then sleep until time to get up and go to work again. It got to be an exhausting grind. Just eat, sleep, and work... and write whenever I could fit in a few minutes here and there.

My writing was going nowhere. I jumped from one genre to another, trying to determine what I was the best at, and found out that I really wasn't very good at any of them at all. Men's adventure, suspense, detective, science fiction, western... I tried them all and failed miserably. I went through several agents – the kind you paid a fee for them to even look at your work – but none could do anything for me.

I began to grow bitter and angry. I regretted taking the path I had chosen, believing that I should have done my best to pursue college or even a trade school of some kind. Dead end jobs came and went. Home felt like a prison, only a place to eat and sleep, and to toil at the ineffective prose that came to mind. It became a vicious cycle and anxiety and depression set in. I became withdrawn and introverted. I had panic attacks whenever I was around strangers or found myself in large crowds.

My interest in Civil War history grew around that time. I spent my weekends away from the typewriter and hiked the battlefields of Murfreesboro and Franklin. It was on a lonesome trail at Stones River Battlefield that I had my one and only ghostly encounter, or so I believe it to be. It was on a balmy spring day in May and, as I traveled the trail, with boulders and heavy thicket to either side of me, I got the strongest sensation that I was no longer alone. It felt as though a presence surrounded me, walking step by step with me, like men on the march. There were other feelings as well; fear and anticipation of something potentially life-threatening to come. It was like I was marching with a unit of soldiers on their way to battle, eager to fight, but also terrified of dying. The sensation grew oppressive and nearly overwhelming.

Then I came to a bend in the trail and stopped in my tracks. I had the sensation that, if I proceeded and passed that curve in the pathway, I would see something I didn't want to see. So, I turned around and started back up the trail... and the sensation of mass presence simply vanished. It was just me in the woods and me alone. When I got back to the trailhead, I got in my car and drove away, and didn't return there for several years. I often wonder what I would have seen if I had chosen to take that bend in the trail.

I also took up black powder shooting. I bought several cap and ball pistols – a .44 Colt Army and a .36 Navy revolver – as well as Kentucky and Hawken rifles I bought as kits and built by hand. I would drive down to Grandmama's farm on the weekends, load my guns the old-fashioned way, with powder, patch, ball, and percussion caps. The odor of burnt powder and tallow grease grew familiar, even comforting, to me. Sometimes I would strap on my pistols and roam the forests of the Spicer property with rifle in hand. It was an escape; transporting me to a different, simpler time. The typewriter slowly became a stranger and my interest in writing began to diminish.

As I entered my early twenties, I lived the macho life; proving my manhood with guns, knives, and the tools and weapons of survivalism. I took a gunsmithing course through correspondence and began to repair guns and build my own hunting knives. My arsenal began to grow to nearly obsessive proportions. A .357 Magnum here, a combat shotgun there, a Ruger Mini-14 assault rifle stashed beneath my bed. Martial artist paraphernalia, too: sai, katana, throwing stars, and nunchucks that would bust your balls if you got careless with your routine.

It was around that time that I became what you would call 'a good old boy', just a step or two away from being downright redneck. It was the era of the Dukes of Hazard, and it wasn't considered shameful to embrace the Confederate flag back then. I displayed them proudly; on my bedroom wall, the license plate on the bumper of my car, on t-shirts and belt buckles. I saw it as harmless. No thought of racism whatsoever; just Southern pride and nothing more. It was later on, when my mother was diagnosed with lung cancer, that I finally saw the error of my ways. While in the hospital, my mother asked me to stop wearing my rebel flag belt buckle, because she was afraid the black nurses would treat her badly if they saw me wearing it. It was the first time that I realized such a symbol might hurt or offend someone. I took the buckle off and never put it on again. Put away the Stars and Bars, and turned my back on that redneck "lost cause" mentality that had possessed me during those stubborn and troublesome years.

I began to focus on my writing again. Around 1981 or 82, I continued to try my luck with the western market. I wrote two novels, *The Last Battle of Reb Bowen* and *Timber Gray.* I sent them to the Scott Meredith Literary Agency in New York City for representation. They didn't make the grade. I did my best not to be discouraged, though. In 1983 I decided to pursue an ambitious writing journey that spanned a grueling two years in length. After reading Brian Garfield's 477 page door-stopper western novel, *Wild Times*, I decided to revive my comic book hero, Dead-Eye, in a lavish western odyssey through the Old West and

RONALD KELLY

make my mark as a published author in that manner. As it turned out, *The Saga of Dead-Eye,* became something of an obsession during the writing process and reached a bloated, overindulgent 880 type-written pages. Needless to say, my agent was unwilling to submit such an ambitious (and, yes, I admit, crudely plotted and written) tome to the western publishers, when they were accustomed to releasing quick-reads of 120 to 150 pages. So, once again, Dead-Eye was shuffled back to the dark tomb of the cedar chest to await another chance in the future.

Around 1986, my interest turned to horror fiction once again and I decided to focus my efforts on breaking into that genre. I was beginning to run out of options and I knew I had to find something that I would be successful at... or simply stop trying at all. It was a last ditch effort.

As it turned out, it was the best decision I could have made at that point in time. Although I didn't know it at the time, returning to my roots, my childhood love of monsters and the macabre, proved to be my salvation.

My Ten Favorite Movies (Non-Horror)

1. To Kill A Mockingbird (1962)
2. Raiders of the Lost Ark (1981)
3. The Outlaw Josey Wales (1976)
4. Planet of the Apes (1968)
5. Avengers: Infinity War (2018)
6. Avengers: End Game (2019)
7. The Wizard of Oz (1939)
8. First Blood (1982)
9. The African Queen (1951)
10. Deliverance (1972)

Chapter Ten

Southern-Fried Horror

I attribute my decision to try my hand at writing horror fiction to one publication; David Silva's *The Horror Show*.

I came upon a copy in 1985 on a magazine rack at *The Great Escape*, a well-known comic book shop in downtown Nashville. I bought it, took it home, and read it. I was unfamiliar with the writers in its table of contents, but it wasn't long before I became immersed in the small press horror scene and began to realize that this periodical published cutting edge horror fiction from some of the best in the business, such as Dean Koontz, Robert R. McCammon, Joe R. Lansdale, and Charles Grant, as well as up-and-coming contributors like Bentley Little, Elizabeth Massie, Poppy Z. Brite, Brian Hodge, and Steve Rasnic Tem.

Nearly all of the horror writers I read during that period possessed a distinct voice and style that was all their own. I knew to be successful, I should strive to do the same. But what was the key? What would be the factor that differentiated me from all the others?

As it turned out, I didn't have to look any further my own back yard. My love for the South, its places and its people, that was the seasoning I would use to flavor my prose. So, I sat down and began to write tales of horror set in my home state of Tennessee, as well as other states south of the Mason-Dixon Line. I drew inspiration from many sources; Southern history, folklore, rural cryptids and legends. I injected the down-home personality and dialect of my family members and neighbors into the characters I constructed and used familiar locales in my settings, both based in my home territory and places I had visited in the deep South; the timbered hills and wooded hollows, lonesome country backroads, small rural towns, and the fetid swamps of Louisiana with their waterlogged cypress and stringy curtains of Spanish moss. Very few writers were writing Southern horror at that time, other than Joe Lansdale and Robert McCammon, so my tales seemed to bring something fresh and new to the table in the small press community.

I began writing stories and submitting them to *The Horror Show*. It was my goal to place a piece of fiction there, but unfortunately I never did. David was always graceful and helpful in his rejection letters, but I always missed the mark. I located potential markets in directories like Janet Fox's *Scavenger's Newsletter* and the SPWAO (Small Press Writers/Artists Organization,) newsletter published by Marge Simon. These directories told which small press magazines were accepting submissions and how much they paid, as well as their individual guidelines. Of course, these were independent publications, not professional ones, so sometimes you only got paid as little as twenty bucks for a story or only in copies of the magazine.

I began to submit stories to many of the leading small press mags at that time – *Grue, Deathrealm, 2AM, Noctulpa* – and sold my first story, "Breakfast Serial" to a little magazine called *Terror Time Again.* I remember the elation I felt when I got that little twenty-five page magazine in the mail; the sense of accomplishment and vindication I felt proud, finally being a published author. The next morning, I took it into work and showed it to my boss. He said, "Did you cut this out of the magazine?" Embarrassed, I said, "Uh, no... this *is* the magazine." So, the wind was knocked of my inflated ego rather quickly and I knew that, for some folks, publication was only legitimate in the sort of manner and presentation that they were accustomed to.

Soon, things picked up quickly and I began to sell my work at an alarming rate. I found myself a regular in a number of small press alongside writers like Elizabeth Massie, Bentley Little, Wayne Allen Sallee, and David Niall Wilson. It reached the point where I actually had fiction appear in thirteen magazines in the span of one year. My reputation grew as a solid and dependable storyteller; one that readers were eager to read. It was an exciting time and I experienced a "writer's high" with each and every story that saw print.

It was around that time that I developed a friendship with a young, fresh-out-of-college writer from Maryland by the name of Richard Chizmar. We would correspond with one another and call one another up on the phone (there was really no internet to speak of in the late1980s). I remember during a conversation one evening he said, "You know, I'm seriously considering starting my own magazine." Thus, *Cemetery Dance* was born. I submitted work to Rich and was fortunate enough to earn a spot in the first issue, as well as numerous issues afterward.

It was around 1989 when the Hat came into the picture. The Hat was my visual signature... my trademark. A gray felt slouch hat reminiscent of those worn by Civil War officers, but with a rattlesnake skin hatband. The Hat appeared in my promotional photos back then; in *Cemetery Dance Magazine*, my short-lived newsletter, *The Fear County Chronicle*, and book section articles in *The Nashville Banner*, *The Tennessean*, and *Nashville Life Magazine.* You never realize the impact of a little thing like how you look or what you wear in this business, how it strikes a chord with readers and fellow authors, until you get out in public and present yourself. During the opening night of the first World Horror Convention in 1991, I didn't wear the Hat and nobody knew me. The following day, I did wear it and *everyone* knew me. It accompanied me on many a book signing and personal appearance, and remained a fixture in my persona as a published Southern writer... until the point where I no longer considered myself one at all. But that comes later.

As I cultivated my individual style and voice, and begin to sell not only to the small press magazines, but well-known, professionally published anthologies as well, I began to draw more and more on my upbringing and the stories my Grandmama Spicer had told me from her rocking chair. Several of her tales inspired stories of my own; *Miss Abigail's Delicate Condition*, *Midnight Grinding*, *Black Harvest*, and *Cumberland Furnace*, to name only a few. I discovered that I had subconsciously adapted her easy and engaging narrative and Southern rural voice, and integrated it into my own storytelling style. In a way, the thing she did best and loved the most lived on through the written word, delivered beyond the front porch to countless readers across the United States and, perhaps, beyond.

Around 1987, I began writing my first horror novel, in hopes that the literary agency I had been submitting to during the previous four or five years would deem it worthy of representing. It wasn't an unusual or unattainable goal for someone in my position, for most of my contemporaries in the small press horror community had similar aspirations; to break away from the pack and make their name in the big leagues, writing for the mass market paperback houses or even major hardcover publishers.

As I labored at the novel, I continued to write for *Cemetery Dance* and dozens of other small press publications. I hoped that this longer work of fiction would be my ticket into the big leagues, and that I would be teleported into the realm of professional writing, where I could quit my day job and make a living doing what I felt I was born to do.

But, as it turned out, it would take a little longer than I initially expected.

Grits & Bits

S **urviving indifference:** Rejection can often seem to be a writers worst enemy, but hard work and persistence can close the gap between being unpublished and being consistently published. There's another foe that is even more daunting... one that attacks your self-esteem, confidence, and even your desire to write. And that nasty bastard is indifference.

No, I'm not talking about your indifference, but that of others. Potential editors and publishers indifference to the work you submit, or, if you are already published, apathetic reactions to your books by reviewers and the reading public. All writers want their work to be read and appreciated (a healthy royalty statement and multi-star reviews don't hurt the ego either). But sometimes you write something that you've really put your heart and soul in and, when it is released, it just sort of lays there, like roadkill on the side of a lonesome highway in the heat of August. No fanfare, no mentions or positive comments on social media (except what you contribute in hopes of generating interest), and poor to non-existent sales from the audience you spent all that time write the book for. Believe me, I've been through it before and it's a rough patch of ground to travel. 2018 was the year it hit me and hit me hard. When my zombie novel, *The Buzzard Zone* was released, it was almost like

I was a figment of my own imagination. No one seemed to notice and no one seemed to care.

So, what do you do? Pout and whine and consider cashing in your chips and quitting? That's what came to my mind and it was an understandable reaction. You may claim that you're writing for your own pleasure and, to a certain extent you are. But, admit it, your main objective is to write stories and novels for other folks to read and enjoy. There could be several reasons for that disheartening lack of interest. Maybe your fiction hasn't reached the point where it is appealing enough to excite readers or you haven't proven yourself in the traditional paying markets and made a name for yourself (I've seen this happen to self-published authors before). Maybe you just haven't connected with your audience yet. Sometimes it takes a lot of hard work and tenacity to hang in there and wait until your readership takes hold and begins to build. Or maybe the type of subject matter you are tackling doesn't suit your voice. If you're particularly good at vampire stories, maybe you completely suck at werewolf tales. Every writer has their strengths and weaknesses; concentrate on what you're good at and go from there. Sometimes a new release is swallowed up by the white noise of too many books coming out during the same period of time. I've had books come out the same week that five or six other big releases hit Amazon. So many writers are trying their hand at the horror genre these days that the competition is fierce. "Oh, but we're not doing this to compete," some in the community exclaim. "We're all here to support one other." Well, that's a nice sentiment, but the fact is, writing and selling books *is* a competitive action. It's business, pure and simple, and whether you admit it or not, you'd really like to sell enough copies to pay the electric bill or take your family to the beach for the weekend.

True, indifference to your work may be disappointing – even devastating – but don't linger and agonize over it. Shrug it off and move on to the next project. Most of the time, the indifference isn't permanent. Your next book may be the one folks truly enjoy and praise; the one that will earn you that audience and set your career in motion.

Chapter Eleven

The Zebra Years

N ote: the following is a book-by-book account of my six year writing career with Kensington Publishing's Zebra Book horror line. I've done my best to provide insight into the inspiration and writing of each novel, as well as the year-by-year history of the gradual decline of horror fiction in the early nineties and the eventual "mass-market horror implosion" that took place midway through that decade.

HINDSIGHT
Original title: THE TOBACCO BARN
Publication date: January 1990
Emotion: Bittersweet

After writing and publishing short stories of Southern-fried horror in the small press magazines for several years, I finally finished my first horror novel. It was heavily inspired by family history... two aspects in particular. First, my mother's life as a child during the Great Depression and her gift of second sight. And secondly, a brutal triple murder that took place in a rural barn during that time, one of the victims being my mother's teenage cousin. I had heard so many stories about the Depression, the murder case, and my mother's childhood from both my mom and my grandmother that the essence and place of time of the mid-1930s was fully accessible. I had no trouble whatsoever writing about rural life in that tragic and hardscrabble period in American history, since I had relived those times through their words.

I based that first novel on the youthful life of my mother and that brutal mass murder and titled it *The Tobacco Barn*, setting the massacre inside an abandoned tobacco-curing barn. I submitted it to my agent at the time, the Scott Meredith Literary Agency, and waited. It was a long wait. They must have submitted it to every publisher in the alphabet, from A to Z, because, two years later, it was finally accepted by Kensington Publishing for their Zebra Books imprint.

My reaction to the sale? A mixture of elation and worried apprehension. After all, this *was* Zebra Books... the dreaded red-headed stepchild of mass market horror publishing. I knew how my peers in the writing community regarded the big Z, with its hologram images, foil embossed titles, and -- heaven forbid -- those tacky skeletons. Even after I had become an established Zebra author, I still carried around the stigma of being a Zebra "horror hack". During the first World Horror Convention, before a panel on Regionalism in Horror, Charles Grant looked over at me and said, "You know, I've read your stuff. It's damn good. So... why the hell are you writing for Zebra?"

I guess the one that was most excited about that first novel sale was my mother. It wasn't because the book was loosely based on her life or that it was a dark tale of horror and suspense... her very favorite type of fiction. No, it was because it was something we both had been looking forward to for a very long time. She was my biggest supporter and to see this happen for her firstborn son was something she relished with great pride and joy. "You're doing it," she told me excitedly. "You're actually going to be a published author!"

Then, almost immediately after the sale, the bad times came. My mother was diagnosed with lung cancer (she had never smoked a cigarette in her life, but had grown up around smokers most of her childhood and in the Nashville textile mill she had worked in before marrying my father). A difficult surgery took place in February of 1989 and, for a while, she seemed to recover completely. Then in the fall of that year it came back with a vengeance. She began to spend more time in the hospital than at home and her weight dropped away drastically. I urged her to read the typewritten manuscript of *The Tobacco Barn* (by then retitled *Hindsight* by the powers that be in the Zebra editorial ranks). But she refused. "I want to read it as a real book," she told me. "I want to hold it in my hands and smell the ink and paper and just devour it...knowing that it came from your imagination and your heart."

But, as it turned out, she never did. As September passed into October, she grew sicker and horribly frail. She went to the hospital for the very last time and never came home. The cancer that ravaged her body took hold of her brain in early November and she began to fade. Her last words to me before lapsing into a coma: "Look at all the pretty flowers!" Later, I would wonder if she had caught a glimpse of Heaven, or had foreseen her own funeral... because every wall of that funeral home ended up covered with flower arrangements from the people who loved her the most, which were many.

A month after her passing, Zebra sent me copies of *Hindsight* several weeks before it hit the bookstores. It was the darkest and loneliest December I ever experienced. But I didn't forsake her memory or the things she loved best. I put up the Christmas tree as always and sat in the darkness, staring at the wink and blink of the colored lights.

In early January, *Hindsight* was released. To say that holding it in my hands was bittersweet would be an understatement. Then came the book signings and the fanfare, and the preparation of my next novel, *Pitfall*, which I had sold to Zebra six months earlier. In time, I learned to love that simple horror novel with the cover of the frightened child in the barn doorway and the disembodied eyes that leered at her from the darkness. And I would think of Mama and wonder if they had a Horror section in the libraries of Heaven.

PITFALL
Original title: PIT DEVILS
Publication date: July 1990
Emotion: Excitement

After I received the call from my agent in early 1989, informing me that Zebra Books had accepted *Hindsight,* I immediately set to work on a second novel in hopes that they might be interested in it, too.

The book was completely opposite of the one I had just written. While *Hindsight* took place in the rural countryside of central Tennessee, *Pit Devils* would be set in the scorching desert of southwestern Texas. Had I ever been there before? Did I have any inkling about the place I was writing about? No... I'd never set foot in the Lone Star State. But I had a solid idea in my head and, throwing caution to the wind, I went for it. I did a lot of research. Tons of it. Mind you, there was no internet to speak of back then; no Google or Bing or Edge to rely on for speedy and accurate information. So, I depended on visits to the local library and my trusty Encyclopedia Britannica... all 32 shelf-bending volumes. Also, I had tried to break, unsuccessfully, into the western genre years before, so this would just be like penning another oater... only with blood, gore, and monsters.

So, why make the carnivorous antagonists of my story Tasmanian devils? There's a funny story behind that. It started years before, probably 1984, during a doctor visit. I was suffering the most hellacious sinus infection I'd ever experienced. While sitting in the waiting room for my turn, I shuffled through some magazines for something to read. There wasn't much to choose from. Newsweek, Woman's Day, and Reader's Digest.

I picked RD and began flipping through it, looking for the joke page. All of sudden, an article caught my eye. It was about Tasmanian devils. Not that pudgy cartoon character that cut through boulders and tree trunks in a cyclone of dust. This was the real deal. I was captivated by the photo beneath the title. It was a vicious, leering little creature with malevolent eyes and the biggest mouthful of razor-sharp teeth I'd ever seen. I skimmed through the article and thought, hey, maybe I could put one of these little devils in a story someday. As a reminder, I... well... I sort of eased that copy of Reader's Digest out of sight of the receptionist at the desk and slyly tore out the page with the photo. Then I secretly tucked it away in my wallet for safe-keeping. Anyway, years later, when I started brainstorming for that second novel idea, I remembered that doctor visit. I rummaged through the papers in my desk and found the page from the Tasmanian devil article and, within an hour, the plot for *Pit Devils* was formed.

It only took me two or three months to write the thing -- on an electric typewriter, no less. After I finished, I made a couple of copies of the manuscript and mailed one to my agent. Three weeks later, he called and said "Guess what? They want this one, too." I was overjoyed, because it totally shot down a doubt that had been nagging at me since I had sold the first novel. Was this all just a fluke? Would *Hindsight* be a one-hit wonder and then it was back to writing those little, short stories for pennies a word? My second acceptance from Zebra told me that it wasn't. All of a sudden, I had multiple books on the release schedule of a major NY publishing house.

Pitfall (again changed from the original title... those know-it-alls in the editorial department were good at that) was released in July of 1990. By then, my emotional state had improved tremendously. Yes, I was still in the grieving process, but I knew the best way to honor my mother's memory was to carry on and build the writing career she had always wanted for me. I gained back the twenty-five pounds I'd lost from worry and stress and arrived at my first *Pitfall* book signing; strong, tanned, and happy.

A note about the cover of *Pitfall*: considering that I was writing for Zebra, the most visually exploitative horror publisher in the business, I had expected savage faces with glowing red eyes and blood-coated fangs, leaping out to terrorize the reader. Instead, it was something totally uncharacteristic for the big Z. It was a simple silver cover with the biggest foil-red Ronald Kelly plastered at the top that I could have ever imagined, especially for a measly second release. You could say that my ego was stoked to capacity and my grin threatened to surpass the boundaries of my ears and meet on the backside of my head. Title and byline fonts like these belonged to greater authors, like King, Koontz, and Straub. To this day, I have no idea what they were thinking at the time. Maybe they believed it would sell more copies. Maybe they thought they would take the high road and be a little classy for a change. Anyway, the novel turned out to be a modest seller, not the blockbuster they probably had hoped for. They probably would have had more lucrative sales if they had done it the plain, old Zebra way and fished something hideous and tacky from the monster pool.

Looking back, I had so much fun writing *Pitfall*. It will always be my "rollercoaster ride" novel, with down to earth characters like Bowie Kane, Lynn Sykes, and Lester Liles and rampaging critters like "hangry" Tribbles with overbites. It was also my last "modest-sized" novel for Zebra. After that, they only grew bigger and more bloated with characters, subplots, and action... for better or worse.

SOMETHING OUT THERE
Original title: THE DARK'UN
Publication date: March 1991
Emotion: Happy and hopeful

Shortly after I received the release date and cover flats for *Pitfall*, Zebra surprised me by offering me a three-book contract. It seemed that the publisher liked my style of writing and the Southern-fried flavor that seasoned it. They wanted to include this backwoods country boy/blue collar welder in their family (or was it stable?) of horror authors and were eager for a long-term relationship. At that point in my career, so was I. The contract didn't offer an obscene amount of money, but it was enough to give me the freedom to concentrate on my prose and the business that went with it. So I quit my job at the welding shop and began to write horror full time.

At that point, I had already started working on another novel. Again, I decided to switch rails and do something completely different from what I had done with *Pitfall*. It was then that I made the decision to write diversely and not lapse into some of the familiar and well-worn Zebra trappings. Many of Z's authors specialized in particular horror tropes that they explored time and time again. Evil children, evil dolls, evil cats, etc. I made a conscious effort from the very beginning not to be pigeonholed. Each novel would be something entirely different from the one before. I had started out with a psychic child during the Great Depression, continued with an outcast Apache handyman fighting a pack of demon-influenced Tasmanian devils, and now I was ready to explore new horrors at a place called Pale Dove Mountain.

The book was originally titled *The Dark'Un*, but of course it didn't stay that way. *Something Out There* was the new nomenclature Zebra gave it and I wasn't all too fond of it. It seemed way too generic for the novel that it represented, in my opinion. The book was set in the mountains of eastern Tennessee and revolved around a small town of decent rural folks, an evil corporation that was bound and determined to do damage in the area for the benefit of greed, and a race of albino changeling creatures that lived nearby on a peak called Pale Dove Mountain. And then there was the Dark'Un; a shadowy and menacing being of folklore that guarded Pale Dove Mountain and protected the albino race... and could turn into some of the most dangerous and deadly creatures and characters imaginable.

Writing this book was a hoot. Actually taking a monster that could have very well been the antagonist and making him a protagonist and champion, both for the albinos and the townsfolk of Tucker's Mill, was somehow satisfying. Yes, the creature did some horrible and gory things, but it was the way a mama bear protects it cubs... except that the Dark'Un could dish out malice and vengeance in the guise of the Frankenstein Monster, a ninja, a Zulu warrior, or a variety of dinosaurs and woodland creatures, just to name a few.

Truthfully, after I finished writing the novel and turned it in, it became something of a headache for the stiff-necked, inflexible editors at Zebra. While my agent absolutely loved it (he actually missed his subway train to Queens sitting in the station, reading the first few chapters), the folks on the editorial staff didn't know exactly what to make of it. Was it horror? Science-fiction? Fantasy? Well, yes, actually it was a little of all of the above. Finally, they realized what I had envisioned, and accepted it as the first novel of the three-book deal.

Before they published the book in early 1991, Zebra sent me the cover flat for *Something Out There*, as they usually did several months before the actual release. It was then that I began to realize that Zebra wasn't all that concerned with how accurate their cover presentation was to the actual novel that was packaged inside. Because whatever that scaly, green, fork-tongued lizard thing coming over the mountain was... it certainly wasn't the Dark'Un and it definitely wasn't a part of my book. (It was also during this period that I came to the realization that a particularly thick skin and taking many things with a grain of salt was a huge part of being a bonified author.)

In January of 1991, my life changed in a very unexpected, but wonderful way. Sit back and get ready for a weird love story.

After my mother's death, my father fell into a deep bout of depression. It lasted through most of 1990 and, by September of that year, began to grow increasingly worse. His grief over my mother's passing preyed on him to the point of him losing weight, sleeping for long periods of time, and calling out of work. It came to the point that I was afraid that I might wake up one morning to find that he had decided to end it all. It reached a critical point and Daddy voluntarily checked into a mental health facility. There he met a woman named Wanda who was suffering from bipolar disorder. They fell in love and married in October of that year. And, abruptly, I had myself a stepmother.

Wanda had a niece named Joyce. When Joyce came to stay with her aunt for a week, we were instantly smitten with one another. Truthfully, it was love at first sight. It didn't seem to matter that I was thirty-one at the time and she was nineteen, or that, technically, we were cousins, although by marriage and not by blood (after all, this *was* Tennessee.) We met on January 10th, were engaged the following Wednesday, and married on January 29th, a mere nineteen days after we first met. A lot of folks who have heard our story think it's bizarre that our courtship was so brief, Some accuse me of robbing the cradle (although artist Alex McVey likes to joke with Joyce, claiming that she was a "grave robber"). But, we've been happily married over thirty-one years now, so we've heard every reaction imaginable to our strange and unconventional romance.

After Joyce and I married, we lived in my hometown of Pegram for several months. We settled into our new life together and my mind returned to my writing and business as usual.

So, I thought, what will the fourth book be about? I had a few ideas lurking around in my head. Maybe a vampire book? A ghost story? Wanting to make the right move, I thought on it for a while. Then late one night, I stepped out on my front porch for a breath of fresh air...

and heard something howl. And it sure as heck didn't sound like a dog.

MOON OF THE WEREWOLF
Original title: UNDERTAKER'S MOON
Publication date: December 1991
Emotion: Confident

So... I was standing on my front porch when I heard the howl.

It was midnight, maybe a little after. I'd been reading most of that night, not writing. I believe it was a book on Irish folklore, although I can't rightfully recall the title. Anyway, my eyes started bothering me and I stepped out on the porch to clear my head and get a breath of fresh air. It was early spring; March I believe. All of the houses on the street were dark... only a streetlight here and there, and a bright, butter-colored moon overhead. I was enjoying the silence and solitude of the hour, when something howled on a tall, wooded hill half a mile away.

It wasn't a dog. Not a coon hound; I'd heard enough blueticks and redbones in my day to know one when I heard one. And it certainly wasn't a stray mutt either. This was something big and loud. *That couldn't be a dog*, I thought to myself. There was something disturbing about it; sad, lonesome, almost tormented. I waited in the darkness, ears straining for sound, listening. But it never came again. I have to admit, a shiver ran up my spine. I went back in, walked to my bedroom, and prepared for bed. The folklore book was still open on my pillow. I was midway through a chapter on banshees and beasties. I thought of that lonesome howl in the night, then turned in for the night.

The next morning I woke up and found a couple of words written on a note pad I kept beside my bed, just in case inspiration struck at some weird and unexpected hour. Apparently, it had. Sometime between midnight and dawn, I had reached over from my slumber and written 'Irish werewolves".

And that was book number four. *Undertaker's Moon*.

Among other subjects, I had always been intensely interested in my Irish heritage and devoured any tome I could find concerning Irish history and folklore. The Kelly family had hailed from the little town of Kiltamagh in County Mayo before immigrating to America and I had always dreamt of going to sweet Erin and walking the green hills and hollows of the place of my ancestry (perhaps someday I actually will.) The thought of combining werewolves, Ireland, and the mortician profession seemed like suitable fodder for a workable and interesting plot. So I went to work and kept my fingers crossed (if you can do that while typing).

Half of the novel I wrote in the country and the other half in the city; Joyce and I decided to move to Nashville and forge a life there, where employment and opportunities were more plentiful. Four months later the book was in the hands of my agent, and then onward to Zebra. It was released under the generic title *Moon of the Werewolf.* The cover wasn't bad... a depiction of a moonlit graveyard with a disembodied werewolf head in the foreground. No raised lettering or foil embossment on this one; none of the usual Zebra bells and whistles. It was a decent enough werewolf tale for that time, I reckon, but it sort of came and went without much fanfare. Being that there was no social media to speak of then, I heard absolutely no feedback about the book whatsoever, except for a review or two in *Locus* and some of the small press horror mags.

I sort of put the werewolf book out of my thoughts and turned my energy on other things. As my novels began to appear on the book racks of drugstores, airport terminals, and bookstore chains like Tower Books, B. Daltons, Waldenbooks, and Books-A- Million, my popularity in the horror genre began to spike. I was invited to submit work to a lot of anthologies around that time... pretty major ones, in fact. Collections like Richard Chizmar's *Cold Blood* and *The Earth Strikes Back*, Joe and Karen Lansdale's *Dark at Heart*, and Thomas Montelone's *Borderlands* series, as well as mass-market horror anthologies like *Shock Rock* and *Hot Blood.* Also an audio collection of a few of my early small press tales titled *Dark Dixie: Tales of Southern Horror* was released by California-based Spine-Tingling Press. The following year it would appear on the nominating ballot of the 1992 Grammy Awards for Best Spoken Word or Non-Musical Album. Not a winner, but it was a huge honor to be considered, nevertheless.

So, with some respectable credits beneath my belt, I settled behind the keyboard again and began to search for the inspiration for my third entry in the multi-book deal.

This time it didn't come with a howl, but a bang.

FATHER'S LITTLE HELPER
Original title: TWELVE GAUGE
Publication date: November 1992

Emotion: Caution

After *Moon of the Werewolf,* I wrote *Twelve Gauge* (eventually retitled *Father's Little Helper* by Zebra). Actually, I wrote TG twice... once in 1982 and then a completely different version in 1991.

The first one came about in a very similar way to *Undertaker's Moon*'s genesis. A sound in the dead of night. It happened way back in February of 1982, a few years after I graduated high school. I was working the night shift on the job I had at the time (I did a lot of that back when I was a young man) and on the nights I had off, I simply kept those weird nocturnal hours and wrote. I was still living at home at the time and was in my bedroom writing (on what, I have no idea. It was probably a western, since I tried to break into that genre, without success, for three or four years). Anyway, it was around midnight or a little past, and I heard a gunshot. Not a pistol shot, but a big throaty boom... a shotgun. A twelve-gauge, I would say. I was a rabid aficionado of firearms at that time, so I knew what most firearms sounded like from the pitch and volume. This one had been fired about a half mile away. Curious, I looked out the bedroom window facing the back yard. There was no moon that night and everything was pitch dark beyond the panes. Past our property was the grounds of Pegram Elementary, a side street, and the little strip mall that housed most of Pegram's businesses. I stared into the darkness for a long moment, but there was no more gunfire. Puzzled, I went back to my writing. A few minutes later, I heard sirens and knew that something bad had taken place.

The next morning I discovered that an off-duty county deputy named Charles Frank Jordan had been called to check out an alarm going off in the drugstore. When he got there, he saw two men inside the pharmacy, looting the shelves for drugs. He crouched behind his car and called for them to exit the premises. A third man, who was acting as a lookout, approached him from behind and shot him in the back with a shotgun as he waited for backup officers. The three suspects, who were brothers, fled the scene but were all apprehended and convicted of felony murder.

The entire community was devastated by the crime. I personally felt saddened and depressed, having heard the fatal shot. It was almost like I had witnessed the whole thing (a writer's imagination can key up his/her emotions like that). A few days later I sat down and began writing *Twelve Gauge*. This version wasn't so much horror as a crime suspense novel. It was pretty straight forward, with Sheriff Ben Gatlin discovering the body of his slain deputy and vowing to bring the culprits to justice. As I remember, I finished it and did absolutely nothing with. Just chucked it away in my filing cabinet and pursued some other writing project.

Later, in 1991, when I was trying to figure out what my fifth novel for Zebra would be, I remembered *Twelve Gauge*. I had been toying with the idea of doing something with a mass murderer or serial killer as the antagonist (I was heavily into true crime nonfiction then) and the general premise of TG seemed to fit the bill. About the only thing I kept from the old novel was the sheriff, Ben Gatlin. As I crafted the plot I began to add other elements; a bloody massacre via twelve-gauge shotgun in a small country church on Christmas Eve, an embittered lawman who had lost his faith at the loss of his wife, and the disturbed son of the mass murderer, who is coached by his dead, executed father to return to the little Tennessee town and finish the job.

As I began to write *Twelve Gauge*, it seemed to grow more and more violent and intense; much more violent that I originally intended it to be. It was one of those strange cases where a work of prose almost takes on a life of its own and follows a dark pathway that you had no idea was even there to begin with. When I finished, I had to admit that it was probably the most brutal and bloody novel I had ever penned.

Of course, Zebra was all for that. They accepted it as the third book in the three-book contract without hesitation. When they sent me the cover flat, I loved the artwork (as well as a very nice blurb from Rich Chizmar at *Cemetery Dance*). But I absolutely HATED the title. *Father's Little Helper* sounded more like a children's book than a horror novel. True, I had used that phrase as the title of Part One inside the book. Leave it to the guys at Z. to grab it and run like hell with it. I disliked the title so much that I called my Zebra editor personally and tried to dissuade him from using it, but no dice.

Around that time, my agent called with an opportunity to ghostwrite for Berkley Books' *Jake Logan* men's western adventure series. The series was written by four or five writers and, apparently, one had passed away or given up their spot. I don't know why, but I hesitated in accepting the offer. Maybe I thought that writing something without my name on the cover was beneath me... that it wasn't exactly legit. I put my agent off for two or three weeks, then finally turned to someone I trusted for advice, especially where the writing business was concerned. And that was Joe R. Lansdale.

I had known Joe for a few years, pretty much since I had appeared on the small press scene back in the late 80s, and he was always supportive and helpful to new writers. In my case, he was very patient and tolerant of a greenhorn horror hack from the sticks who called him up every now and then for advice. Joe had given me my first blurb (which graced the back cover of *Something Out There*) and accepted my story "Beneath Black Bayou" for *Dark at Heart*, which had been published by Dark Harvest earlier that year. When I asked him about the *Jake Logan* opportunity, he told me "I don't see anything wrong with it. I've ghostwritten before. Go for it."

So, with Joe's approval, I contacted my agent and accepted the offer. I ended up writing two novels in the series; *Slocum and the Nightriders* (#174) and *Slocum and the Gold Slaves* (#187). It was a sweet gig. It only took a couple of weeks to write a 180 page book (with three or four sex scenes sprinkled throughout) and you were paid a flat five-thousand per book. Unfortunately, Berkley decided to shut down the *Jake Logan* series shortly after I began writing them. When they finally decided to bring it back, all of the ghostwriting spots had been filled and my side job was over and done with.

In November of '92, *Father's Little Helper* was finally released. It did okay, but didn't sell as well as *Moon of the Werewolf* had. Also, where I'd had two books a year scheduled in 1990 and 1991, there had only been the one in '92. Was this due to a backlog of upcoming releases at Zebra, or something else? Slowly, I was beginning to learn that the state of the horror genre wasn't quite as healthy as it openly seemed to be.

One thing that alerted me was talk, both in the industry and in the retail stores, that mass market publishing in general wasn't doing so hot. Seemingly, the market was being flooded with horror and romance novels to satisfy a growing demand. The trouble was, a whole lot of it was pure, grade-A crap. Folks started buying books and getting burnt by the terrible plotting and writing, convoluted sub-plots and an overabundance of lackluster characters. Soon, the publishers started losing money and started cutting their losses... namely their publishing lines and authors. From all outward appearances, horror had seemed healthy and lucrative. Maybe to the authors it genuinely appeared to be that way. But to the publishers and editors and agents behind the scenes it was different. There were dropping sales figures, staff lay-offs, and schedule delays. I remember a lady that ran a used bookstore (where I did a lot of my signings) talking about romance, fantasy, and horror authors losing their publishers or their genre lines being shut down. Once she asked "How is everything with you, Ron? I mean, have you heard anything negative from your publisher lately?" Truthfully, I told her no... everything was great. But, secretly, I began to suspect that it wasn't.

From that point onward, I proceeded with caution, particularly where my writing career was concerned. I didn't ask my agent or editors any questions because, frankly, I didn't want to give them any ideas. *Father's Little Helper* had been the last book of that three-book contract. Secretly, I began to wonder if I would be fortunate enough to see another one.

THE POSSESSION
Original title: BURNT MAGNOLIA
Publication date: November 1993
Emotion: Frustration

As it turned out, I didn't have to worry... at least not at that point in time. Shortly after Zebra received the manuscript of *Father's Little Helper*, they offered me yet another three-book contract.

This eased a little of my anxiety and doubt. Since they had offered me another multi-book deal, then things were okay, right? As long as they were contractually obliged to publish my work, I had nothing to worry about. As it turned out later, that wasn't how it necessarily works out in the publishing business.

Before the ink was sufficiently dry on the contract, I was already brainstorming for my sixth novel. I was biting at the bit to write a vampire book, but didn't have a premise that I was comfortably confident with. So, I decided to write a ghost story. A Civil War-themed ghost story.

Anyone who knew me back then pretty much expected that to happen. I had always been a huge student and enthusiast of Civil War history. I reckon it was natural, since I was enamored with American history since a small child, particularly the Old West and the War Between the States. My family, on both my mother and father's side, boasted ancestors who had fought for the Union and the Confederacy. And, so with that in mind, I decided to form a plausible storyline.

I titled the book *Burnt Magnolia* (although, of course, it was changed once again by the contrary folks at Z, to the generic moniker *The Possession*). The story involved a popular romance author and her horror artist husband who had moved into a restored Southern ma nsion... a mansion that had suffered a horrible tragedy during the Union Army's occupation of Franklin, TN and was violently and undeniably haunted. The story also involved a homosexual investigator of paranormal phenomenon, an elderly couple who ran the town bookstore, and a young black man in search of his ancestry. After the book was released, a good friend of mine said that this was my first "politically-correct" horror novel, for it featured gays, African-Americans, and the elderly as major characters. I suppose that might have been the case, but it wasn't consciously my intention while writing it. As long a character is interesting and written honestly, I have no qualms or reservations about what race, religion, or sexual orientation they might be.

So, I finished the novel and it was published in November of 1993. I soon became frustrated with the fact that I couldn't find it at some of the bookstores and retail stores that had normally carried my books before. Had this press run been smaller than the others? Had Zebra not given it the promotional push it needed to succeed? Again, those old rumors about the "death of horror" raised its ugly head in the back of my mind. In fact, I couldn't determine how it was received by readers and potential fans at all. One troubling thing about writing for Zebra was the sense of isolation that its authors found themselves experiencing from novel to novel. There was no social media back then, no reader interaction like there is today on Facebook or Twitter. You simply sat there and wrote and hoped (no, prayed) that someone, somewhere would read it and enjoy it. If they did, you didn't hear about it. If they hated it, you didn't hear about it either. It was both exasperating and depressing. If you talked to fellow writers it was by snail mail or phone, and then they seemed just as isolated and out of touch as you were.

Another thing that frustrated me was the apathy that local bookstores showed toward my work and the horror genre in general. Since *The Possession* was set in the actual Tennessee town of Franklin, I contacted Franklin bookstore owners and attempted to set up signings. None seemed particularly excited about the prospect of having a local author sign books in their establishments. "I'm sorry," they would say, "but we don't believe our patrons would be interested in that sort of book." What? A ghost story set in your hometown dealing with the Civil War (which your community embraces and exploits at every opportunity imaginable)? "No," they said, "not interested."

Then there was the big signing I had scheduled with Nashville's Davis-Kidd; probably the city's most popular and prestigious bookstore at that time. I was so stoked and excited to finally get a signing with them. Then a representative called and said "I'm afraid we're going to have to cancel the signing. We can't determine precisely when the release date is." "But you've known the release date for three months," I told them, "and we have a signing date already set." But they would hear no logic on my part and promptly canceled me without further explanation. When the date of my canceled signing rolled around, low and behold, a local celebrity disc jockey (a fixture in Nashville's country music community) just conveniently stepped into my spot, signing hardcovers of his new biography.

Following the release of *The Possession*, I literally felt like I was stuck in neutral, spinning my wheels. Either the booksellers and book-buyers were getting sick of Ol' Ron and his Southern-fried storytelling or people were just growing sick and tired of horror in general. As I prepared to plot out my seventh novel, I felt anxious and desperate. I knew I needed something different ... something special. Something that didn't read or feel like the same old, tired monster book retread. Something that folks would read and remember years later... maybe carry around in their soul for a while. My Magnum Opus, so to speak.

It was a tall order. Something I didn't expect to come easily. Something that was probably unattainable at that point in my career and was practically impossible. But as it turned out, it wasn't nearly as difficult or beyond the bounds of possibility as I first imagined it would be.

FEAR
Original title: FEAR COUNTY
Publication date: September 1994
Emotion: Satisfaction

I had been going through some weird things as a writer at that time. Fear at the thought of losing the career that I had sought and fought for so diligently. Doubt at my own ability to sustain that career and keep coming up with something different and interesting to readers. Weary and nearly burnt out from adhering to Zebra's strict contract stipulations, mainly the "bigger is better, fatter is fabulous" rule. Sometimes a novel wasn't meant to be 450 to 550 pages; sometimes less was more. I found myself struggling to fill in the blanks... to stretch a decently paced storyline into something close to excessive and obscenely bloated. My cast of characters resembled a high school reunion or a comic book convention, instead of a tight ensemble of necessary players. Readers were beginning to grow bored and cheated by the overblown doorstoppers now. I wondered if my next novel would fall into that category and if folks would become tired and disgusted at the extra subplots and characters and stop reading it midway through... or even sooner. I thought of *Hindsight* and *Pitfall* and their modest 200+ pages, and knew that I could never go back there again... not with Zebra.

Then I wrote FEAR.

Don't ask me where I got the idea. I couldn't, for the life me, tell you for sure. It was one of those rare occurrences in a writer's life when the literary planets align perfectly and inspiration strikes like a bolt of lightning. I just sat down and began to write and it started to flow. And it didn't stop or slow down. The cast of characters took on flesh and blood, heart and soul. Farm boy Jeb Sweeny and his shell-shocked father, Sam. The traveling bluesman, Roscoe Ledbetter. The sisters of darkness and light, the Snake Queen and the Granny Woman. And that serpentine creature, the Snake Critter, that had slipped the boundaries of a dark stretch of rural purgatory and reigned terror upon Jeb's hometown. Even Fear County became a character of sorts, with its various horrors and dangers, especially as Jeb and company travel deep into its black heart, in search of the only bit of goodness that existed within its borders.

I had a fondness for coming of age tales around that time; King's *It* and *The Body*, McCammon's *Boy's Life-*, Simmons' *Summer of Night*, just to name a few. I had tried my hand at it with *Hindsight* several years before. Now I was attempting it again, a bit more polished and confident than I had been with the first one. There was very little effort with the storyline or dialogue... everything seemed genuine and unforced. I kept waiting to hit a snag or fall in a plot hole, but it never happened. Quite simply, it was the most satisfying writing experience I'd had up to that point in my career... and it still claims that distinction. A rare creative occurrence that I doubt I will ever experience again.

When I turned the manuscript in as my second offering of that second multi-book deal, I actually felt good about it. Zebra was pleased with the book and seemed to put a little extra effort into getting it out there to the reading public. They shortened the title from *Fear County* to *Fear* (maybe because the former sounded a bit too rural), but that was okay with me. And the cover art was certainly eye-catching with the cocooned children dangling from the ceiling of the cave. Soon, I saw *Fear* everywhere, even places where I'd never seen my books before. And the reviews were extremely favorable, too. During the Zebra years – and even afterward – *Fear* became my bestselling novel and my most well-received.

It did so well, in fact, that Zebra promptly offered me another multi-book contract... two novels this time instead of three... and I still had one to go on the previous one. At that point in my Zebra career, I could see no limit to the number of books I might write for the big Z in the years to come. It looked like I had found my literary niche and I was there to stay.

But, unfortunately, as we all know, looks can often be deceiving...

BLOOD KIN
Original title: BLOOD KIN
Publication date: June 1996
Emotion: Uncertainty

In the spring of 1994, I wrote *Blood Kin*. I had been wanting to write a vampire novel for several years but not the kind that I had been seeing on the book racks. It would be a real, old-school vampire tale, with a truly evil bloodsucker, brought back to life from an unmarked grave and intent on turning the descendants of his namesake into a congregation of the undead. The vampire was Grandpappy Josiah Craven, a 1900's traveling preacher turned Nosferatu. The protagonist was Boyd Andrews, a divorced father and alcoholic down on his luck. Instead of the customary wildlife a vampire could transform into (bats, rats, and wolves), Grandpappy took on the images of the wildlife of his native Tennessee Appalachia (crows, weasels, bears, and wild boars).

I sort of set a new record for myself with that one. I wrote it in two months flat. Started it in March and had it in Zebra's hands by early May. My reason for the speedy delivery? Money. Zebra's multi-book contracts paid out that portion of the advance upon acceptance. And I was desperately in need of greenbacks. My wife and I were struggling to make a life in a suburb of Nashville and times were hard. Writing full-time wasn't the lucrative dream that I had believed it would be. Stephen King, Dean Koontz, and Anne Rice were making the big bucks, while me and the other 99.9% of professional writers were eating fish sticks and cheap macaroni and cheese, and trying to pay the electric bill before the cut-off date. So, I need that money... badly.

Zebra loved *Blood Kin*. I anxiously awaited to hear the release date. When I found out, I wasn't a happy camper. *BK* wouldn't be released until 1996! That meant there would be an entire empty year and a half between *Fear* and the next book. I couldn't understand the delay and, when I asked, I couldn't get a clear answer. So, faced with the prospect of being in publishing limbo for such a long stretch, I started on the books of the third multi-book deal.

The two books were *Hell Hollow* and *Restless Shadows*. *Hell Hollow* was another coming-of-age tale about four pre-teens battling the evil incarnation of Doctor Augustus Leech, a traveling medicine show man who collected souls through the sale of his patented elixir and some magical playing cards that trapped their owners into a land of dreams and nightmares. *Restless Shadows* was the long-awaited sequel to *Hindsight*, in which an elderly Cindy Ann and her granddaughter, Beth (both with psychic abilities) return to the rural town of Coleman after a family is brutally murdered in the same tobacco barn that had hosted a mass murder during the 1930s.

By the time I finished the two books, Joyce and I had moved away from Nashville and out to the country. We rented a little farmhouse surrounded by pastureland, fresh air, and plenty of cows. Zebra readily accepted *HH* and *RS* without hesitation. I soon discovered that they would be released in 1997 and 1998. "Okay," I thought, "just a little hitch in my career and then I'm back on a regular publishing schedule again."

Then the horror genre, as we knew it then, imploded.

Sales slowed to a crawl. Publishers looked at the falling numbers and panicked. Authors began to lose their publishers and publishers began to stop accepting or buying manuscripts, particularly horror. Entire horror lines were being disbanded, right and left. It was a sad time... a scary time. Especially if you made a living off monsters, murderers, and mayhem.

Blood Kin was released in the summer of 1996. It did very well and sold about as well as *Fear* had. It fetched nice reviews and spent quality time on alot of paperback racks. So, I thought maybe I had nothing to worry about. I mean, if your book sells well, they're not going to want to dump you, are they? I did my best to convince myself that I was one of the exceptions... that it wouldn't happen to me.

But I had already sensed that it was a possibility. I had sent outlines to my Zebra editors for new books, trying to net a new multi-book deal. But they wouldn't bite. "Not exactly up to par" they would say, or "let's see how the next two books do and then we'll talk." I could tell that they were stalling... that they were just stringing me along.

But I didn't know why... until autumn rolled around.

My Twelve Favorite RK Mythos Heroes & Heroines

1. Jeb Sweeny | *Fear*
2. Cindy Ann Biggs | *Hindsight, Potter's Field, Restless Shadows*
3. Roscoe Ledbetter | *Fear*
4. Boyd Andrews | *Blood Kin*
5. The Granny Woman | *Fear, The General's Arm*
6. Ian Danaher | *Undertaker's Moon*
7. The Dark'Un | *The Dark'Un* aka *Something Out There*
8. Bowie Kane | *Pitfall*
9. Dead-Eye | *The Saga of Dead-Eye*
10. Job | *The Saga of Dead-Eye*
11. Jeremiah Springer aka Hot Pappy | *The Seedling, Beneath the Branches*
12. Diarmuid O'Sheehan | *O'Sheehan!*

Chapter Twelve

The Long Hiatus

I t happened on the 6th of October 1996. My own personal 9/11.

I was working on a short story that afternoon. Joyce was working for an insurance company in downtown Nashville at the time, sixty miles from home. At 3:47 the phone rang (funny how I remember exactly what time it was).

It was my agent at Scott Meredith. *Finally!* I thought to myself. *It's about time Zebra got off their ass and gave me some good news!* But, as it turned out, it wasn't exactly the call I had hoped for.

"I have news," he said.

"Okay," I answered. Something in his voice unsettled me.

He hesitated for a moment and then sighed. "It's not good news."

The next five minutes seemed to last an agonizing eternity. As my agent began to explain the situation, I felt as though I had been gut punched by a runaway freight train.

Zebra Books was doing away with their horror line. No more gruesome in-your-face covers, no more 500

141

pagers. Everything was kaput... out of the picture. And with it, dozens of authors who depended on them to pay their mortgage and keep their families fed.

"But they're still going to release the last two books, aren't they?" I asked. No. *Hell Hollow* and *Restless Shadows* would be returned to me and, since Zebra had defaulted on the contract, I would keep all advance money that had already been paid.

"But, we can try someone else, can't we?" I asked frantically. "I mean, I've published eight novels. That should count for something, shouldn't it?"

"I'm sorry," he said, "but I don't think finding you another publisher is an option right now," he told me. "My advice to you is to keep writing... but write anything *but* horror. It's pure poison right now."

When I hung up, I simply stood there for a few minutes, feeling stunned and disoriented. I remember walking onto the front porch of the farmhouse and sitting in a rocking chair until my wife got home that evening from her job. She knew something bad had happened when she got out of the car. "What's wrong?" she asked. She must have thought there had been a death in the family. In an odd way, there had.

"It's all gone," I told her. "Everything. Gone." As a Southern man, I had been raised to believe that tears and emotion were weaknesses. But at that moment I practically fell into my wife's arms and cried for what seemed to be hours.

I had struggled with anxiety and depression when I was a teenager. It all came back, full force, as autumn fell away and the chill of winter set in. I tried to take my agent's advice... tried to write and sell to other genres. But it seemed hopeless. Doors remained closed and my mailbox grew heavy with rejection slips.

I lost my resolve and was sure that everything had turned out as it had for a reason. Being a Christian man,

I began to believe that maybe God had ended my career; that He wasn't pleased with what I was writing and had brought the whole thing crashing down upon my head. I don't believe that now, but I did back then. So I just stopped. Stopped writing and stopped trying. Stopped reading horror fiction of any kind. In my mind, I'd had my shot and blown it, although through no fault of my own.

So, I laced up my steel-toed boots, packed my lunch box, and went back to work. Made my living in the factories, just as I had before I had published that first short story. I had books on my bookshelf with my name on the covers and spine, but it was difficult to even look at them and remember what I had achieved and lost in such a short period of time.

I found a job in nearby Gordonsville, running a shell press for a company that manufactured electric motors for elevators and Jacuzzis. I worked the seven to three shift, loved my wife, and began to raise a family. And I did that for ten long years. Just Ol' Ron Kelly the blue-collar worker, drawing a paycheck and putting the callouses back where they used to be. The Ron Kelly that wrote novels and had met and rubbed elbows with the likes of Robert Bloch, Charles Grant, Karl Edward Wagner, and Richard Matheson was ancient history... non-existent... dead and gone.

It was a year and half before I got the rights back from Kensington for *Hindsight, Pitfall,* and *Something Out There.* It was another year before *Moon of the Werewolf, Father's Little Helper,* and *The Possession* were securely

143

in my possession again. But, for some reason, they refused to relinquish the rights to my bestsellers, *Fear* and *Blood Kin.* Not that it mattered much to me. I filed the "Return of Literary Rights" letters in a desk drawer and forgot about them. That was ancient history to me at that point. I had a good job, health insurance, and, for the first time since leaving my hometown of Pegram, stability that didn't involve haunting the mailbox daily in hopes of finding a royalty check there to pay the water and electric bills.

In 1989, Joyce and I had our first child; a daughter named Reilly. I was now a father and my responsibilities had increased to a point where a full-time job was

absolutely necessary. Even if I'd had aspirations of returning to writing, there was no turning back now. I was a working man with a wife and a child and, like my father before me, I had an obligation to devote all my time and energy in providing for them the very best I could.

Around the fifth year of my long hiatus, I began to grow increasingly unsatisfied and irritated, especially in the shadow of my past occupation. I would come up with an idea for a story or novel out of the blue and immediately cast it from my mind. *Don't be dwelling on stuff like that,* I would tell myself. *It's over and done with. You're just making yourself miserable.* I packed up the Zebra books and stashed them out of sight, like they had never existed. The Hat with its rattlesnake skin band sat atop my bookcase, gathering dust. Eventually, I could bear the sight of it no more. I ended up selling it in a yard sale for ten bucks.

In the years 2000 and 2001, I finally discovered the reason why Kensington had refrained from returning the last rights to my work to me. Under the Pinnacle imprint, they rereleased both *Fear* and *Blood Kin.* Both sold very well – perhaps even better than they had the first time around. The royalties were very welcome and provided us the opportunity to add another daughter, Makenna, to the family in 2004.

It was around that time, that I began to realize that I was only hurting myself in denying who I was and what I had accomplished from 1986 to 1996. I remember getting up the courage to unpack my Zebra novels and take them to work in my lunch box, to show some of my co-workers. I recall that my line leader at the time, Angela Gibbs, walked up to my press one afternoon with a look of amazement on her face, and asked "Are you actually a published author?" The word seemed foreign to me at first... like the hazy remnants of a dream I'd had a long time ago. I finally nodded and said "Yeah... I *was*. But not anymore."

A couple of years passed. More and more, the thought of trying my hand at writing crossed my mind. But I kept putting it off, telling myself it was pointless to consider the possibility. I had been away from the horror genre for a decade. To attempt to return to it after so long an absence would only be setting myself up for bitter disappointment and failure.

But fate has a way of throwing you a curve ball sometimes... and gives you one more shot to knock it out of the park.

And, so, in the summer of 2006, the decision was practically made for me... by several folks that I didn't even know at the time.

Five Lessons I Learned While Working With Mass Market Publishing

Read your contracts thoroughly - It is very easy for a new (and especially unpublished) author to jump into a publishing agreement without weighing their options or fully understanding the various clauses and stipulations that are being presented to them. Most mass market publishing contracts can be between eight and twelve pages in length, and full of legal jargon the author doesn't fully understand. If you don't understand or are uncertain of particular passages, seek out the assistance of a literary agent or an attorney who deals with creative and literary properties. Don't be afraidthat the publisher will cancel the deal if you question or wish to change certain things in the contract (this is a mistake of a lot of authors make; believing that this is their only chance for publication and that a publisher will terminate the offer if anything in the contract is questioned or challenged). At the same time, most stipulations in mass market contracts are standard practices and a novice author making unreasonable demands can cause friction between the two parties before a publishing relationship has even begun.

Work through a literary agent - Submitting manuscripts and building and retaining a working relationship with a publisher through a qualified literary agent is a positive advantage when dealing with large publishing houses. An agent knows who is looking for particular genre properties and works in the author's favor, as far as percentage of royalties, press run numbers, and additional acquired rights such as e-book, audiobook, and foreign sales. When working with Zebra, I found my agent to be invaluable as far as keeping me in the loop with publication schedules and the collection and disbursement of royalties. They are also street savvy when it comes to contracts and how they favorably or unfavorably affect their client. I remember receiving contracts from Zebra that had large sections blacked out and excluded; sections that I would have probably blindly accepted, but my agent had the wisdom and knowledge to reject in my behalf.

Retain creative control - One of the most annoying and infuriating things about my relationship with Zebra Books was my loss of creative control and say-so when it came to the publication of my novels. My two biggest pet peeves was the almost inevitable changing of my titles (usually to some bland and generic title that would appeal to a wider purchasing public)and the cover design and artwork for my books. Since Zebra had creative control over those aspects of my novels,

I had little or no leverage in retaining the original titles or make creative suggestions on how the books would be packaged and promoted. Of course, during that era of mass market publishing, it was normally the publisher's right and prerogative to make such creative decisions, usually at an editor's discretion or by editorial committee. If at all possible, attempt to control the amount of creative license the publisher has with the publication and presentation of your work. This is usually no problem with the independent presses (who will normally retain your original title and are open to cover and design suggestions), but that is normally not the case with the big publishing houses.

Beware of multi-book deals - Multi-book deals can be advantageous for an author... up to a certain point. I had three such agreements during my tenure at Zebra and, for the most part, they gave me a degree of security and provided the means to write full-time for nearly six years. However, there were pitfalls to being bound to such restrictive contract. Let's say you sign a three-book deal, and after the publication of the first book, your career skyrockets. You do not have the clear and free option to submit your next work to various publishers; you are bound by contract to write and deliver the next two books to your current publisher, before you are released from the agreement. I would say it is probably preferable to sign multi-book deals when it comes to a particular series of books (I've done so with Thunderstorm and Silver Shamrock), but think twice when it comes to stand-alone novels.

Don't put all your eggs in one basket - When Kensington shut down the Zebra Horror line in 1996, I found myself in an extremely precarious situation. I was completely without a publisher and, since I depended on Zebra as my sole source of income, I was also unemployed. That, in itself, was the most valuable lesson

RONALD KELLY

I learned from my time as a mass market paperback author. Never put all your eggs in one basket. Refrain from devoting all of your present and future publications to one publisher. It is best to divide your writing projects between a number of publishing houses, which is much easier if you are concentrating on the indie market, rather than major paperback and hardcover publishers. Currently, I have five publishers I work with on a regular basis, and four or five more if you count contributions to anthologies. Plus, the small press has its advantages. It's sort of like the Hydra of Greek legend; if one publisher folds, two more will take its place.

Chapter Thirteen

Prodigal Son

In the mid-nineties, I made friends with a guy named Mark Hickerson. This was around 1994, or a little afterward, because I remember receiving a long, eight-page fan letter from him praising *Fear* and all my other novels up to that point. We were living in Nashville at the time and Mark and his wife lived in Manchester, only forty miles away, so we invited them down for a visit. It wasn't long before we became close friends.

Mark was there during the final years of my stint with Zebra and provided much-needed support when everything crashed and burned. Even during the long stretch of ten years afterward, Mark always had faith in me, He never lost hope of me returning to writing, even when I felt no hope at all.

Every now and then, Mark would give me a pep talk and try to get me motivated. Around 2003 and 2004, he was particularly adamant. "Horror is booming again, man!" he told me. "This new guy, Brian Keene... he's written a zombie book and it's revitalized the genre. You really need to consider getting back into it."

But, unfortunately, I was turning deaf ears to his advice. "That's all a done deal for me, Mark," I would reply with a sigh (yes, I actually sighed). "I don't have any interest in writing again."

But, of course, that was a lie. I *was* considering it... very seriously. But I reckon I was too gun-shy to do anything about it. The disaster with Zebra had been devastating on an emotional level. To achieve your dream of becoming a published mass market author and then have it literally ripped away from you in a relatively short period of time was traumatic... and I would be damned if I was going to go through it all over again. So, I continued to take the safe route and avoid writing and reading horror fiction entirely. Besides, I had been away from the genre for a decade. In my mind, it would be like starting all over again and I wasn't sure I still had the desire to do that, considering it took me twelve years to accomplish that feat the first time around. It was less hurtful to simply refrain from taking that chance and, basically, acting like my first writing career had been a fluke, or even worse, never happened at all.

But Mark simply wouldn't leave it be. Maybe he saw something that I didn't; that the chance for a comeback was there and that maybe it wouldn't be as difficult as I imagined. To tell the truth, it grew annoying at times, his constant suggestions and insistence, but, on reflection, I know it was only because I was being too damned stubborn to listen. I had grown too comfortable and complacent in the mediocrity of a decade's worth of working in the factories and feeling sorry for myself.

In the summer of 2005, Mark came back from Hypericon in Nashville with a stack of books. Leisure horror paperbacks that were all signed to me... all from authors who actually seemed to know who I was. A couple were from writers I weren't familiar with – Bryan Smith and James Newman – but there were several from the guy Mark had mentioned before...

Brian Keene. I opened a novel titled *The Rising* and read the inscription on the title page. *Thanks for the years of inspiration!* it said in blood-red ink. So, all those books I had written years ago hadn't been for nothing after all. People had read them and somehow been inspired by them to try their hand at writing as well.

Now, you would think something like that would light a fire under my ass. It should have, but it didn't. I was still the hermit, hiding in the cave of self-pity, afraid to come out. I set those books on my shelf – books written by authors who held me and my work in such high regard – and didn't read them. Just let them gather dust and forgot all about them. In other words, I was a complete and utter dumb-ass.

Another year passed. Mark was uncharacteristically silent. No pep talks... no rallying me toward a fresh, new career in the horror genre. I figured maybe he had finally gotten the message; that Ron Kelly was stuck flat in neutral. He wasn't going forward to the vast unknown of a genre that had crumbled and slowly rebuilt itself, and he certainly wasn't looking over his shoulder at a past that had been bright and golden for a brief while, then imploded with one afternoon phone call from NYC.

Then in May of 2006, Mark called me up again. "Dude, they're talking about you over on Robert McCammon's message board!"

Now, I had been a huge fan of Robert R. McCammon when I was reading and writing in the 80s and 90s. *Boy's Life* was my all-time favorite coming-of-age novel and as an author from the South, he had been a major inspiration, along with down-home scribes like Joe Lansdale and Manly Wade Wellman. So my interest was piqued. "So," I asked, "what are they saying?"

"You know, they're talking about how great your books were and wondering what happened to you. Asking if you were dead or not."

Dead? That sort of sucker punched me in the gut a little. In their eyes, maybe I was. Maybe the sudden and inexplicable disappearance of that Zebra author who had written dark Southern tales like *Fear, Blood Kin, Hindsight,* and *Moon of the Werewolf* had sounded like a death knell... like the hammering of ten-penny nails in the lid of a casket. Undoubtedly, that's what I had been thinking for the last ten years, and I was the poor bastard that had been lowered six feet under and covered over with the sod of bitterness and bad breaks. While folks were out there, still finding my battered paperbacks in used bookstores and wondering what had become of me, I was gasping for air in the darkness, prematurely buried by my own foolish hand.

After Mark's phone call, I admit, I was rattled. Out of curiosity, I wanted to rush right over and read what those readers – maybe even *fans* – had been saying about me. The problem was... I had no computer. The internet had been in its infancy when I had stopped writing, so I hadn't exactly advanced with the rest of the world. I had moved to the country, put everything but work and family out of my mind, and was completely ignorant of the wonders of cyberspace and the Information Highway.

Joyce agreed to pull McCammon's website up at work and print me off the thread concerning me and my writing career. The following day, she came home with a big grin on her face and twenty-seven printed pages of posts and comments. When I sat down to read them, I felt something stir inside me. It was like someone had journeyed into the depths of a deep, dark cave, jabbed a sleeping grizzly with a pointy stick, and said "Wake up, you lazy son of a bitch! You've been hibernating way too long!"

For an hour, I read and reread those posts, praising my work and lamenting my absence from the horror scene. One comment in particular hit a nerve. It was from a fellow named James Newman (now where had I heard that name before?). He said: "I heard that he's working in a factory now. That he stopped writing completely. That's really sad."

I sat there for a long moment and thought about it. *Damn*, I told myself, t*hat is sad.* Sure, what had happened to me back in '96 had been terrible, but what I had done to myself in the ten years afterward had been infinitely worse. I'd become disillusioned with the publishing industry and turned my back on my love for writing , as well as my love for the genre that had pretty much nurtured and carried me through childhood and into young adulthood.

That weekend, I went to my bookshelf and took down Brian Keene's *The Rising.* I found it unorthodox, relevant of the times, and refreshing; similar in impact to the work of Jack Ketchum or early Stephen King, but with a down-to-earth, blue collar feel. And that ending! Talk about a cliffhanger! *What the shit did he do that for?* I wondered. Or, more importantly, *How the hell did he get away with it?* Needless to say, I sat down and read *City of the Dead* the same weekend... and have considered myself a die-hard Keene aficionado ever since.

The next one I decided to sample was *Midnight Rain.* Again, the name on the spine haunted me. Then that comment on the McCammon site slapped me in the face. *"I heard that he's working in a factory now. That he stopped writing completely. That's really sad."* I settled into a chair on the front porch, cracked that sucker open, and began reading. *Okay, Mr. Newman,* I thought, *let's see what you have to show me.* And, boy, did he show me plenty. After I finished, I honestly felt as though I had come to a long-awaited revelation. *I think I can do this again! Maybe I should seriously consider giving this gig a second chance.*

The following day, Joyce and I drove to Best Buy and bought an HP desktop. Soon, I was logging onto the McCammon message board and interacting with those who had commented on my books – and my whereabouts – several days before. To say that my appearance online was surprising and the response was positive is a bit of an understatement. Soon, strangers became friends and I was being urged to return to the horror genre and continue what I had started years before.

I talked it over with Joyce and, excitedly, she encouraged me to give it another try. So, the next morning I started a new thread on the McCammon board and officially announced that I was returning to the horror genre.

And, almost immediately afterward, realized what I had done and was scared shitless. *You idiot!* I told myself, *here you've done gone and made this grand* entrance, and you haven't written a damn word in ten years!

But, as it turned out, my fears were unfounded. I sat down and wrote the first short story I had written since 1996 and it was like I had never left. It simply flowed...maybe even better than it had before.

Folks started getting wind of my return and the first phone call I received was from an old friend. Richard Chizmar, my buddy from the small press days, had gone from magazine editor to respected independent publisher during my hiatus. Just hearing his voice again put me at ease and enforced my suspicions that maybe I had done the right thing after all. "Hey, buddy!" he said. "It's great to have you back. So... what would you like to do?"

I told him that I would like to release a novel and my first short story collection. Before that phone call was over, the deal had been made. Cemetery Dance Publications would publish *Hell Hollow*, my previously-scheduled (by Zebra), but yet unpublished coming-of-age novel, and *Midnight Grinding: Tales of Twilight Terror,* a whopping thirty-two story collection, focusing on my small press and anthology short fiction between 1988 and 1996. They would end up being my first works in hardcover.

Also at that time, I struck up a friendship with Hunter Goatley, an aficionado of Superman, Kiss, Alice Cooper, and Planet of the Apes who had designed Robert McCammon's website and served as its administrator. He offered to design a site for me and, soon, RonaldK elly.com was born. Hunter was the first one to coin the phrase "Southern-Fried Horror". He included it on the banner of my website from day one and, upon seeing it, I thought "Yeah, let's stick with that." And that's how I've classified my style of down-home, rural fiction from then on.

So, just like that, I was back in the fold again. I have several people I owe a debt of gratitude for dragging me from the edge of the abyss and back in front of the keyboard. Brian Keene and James Newman for inspiring me with their work and putting my creative wheels into motion, and Rich Chizmar for opening the door and giving me the opportunity to publish again. But, truth be told, it really all comes down to one person. The one who was most instrumental in bringing me back to the horror genre was Mark Hickerson.

Shortly after I had made the two book deal with Cemetery Dance, Steven Lloyd (Barnes), an editor at Nocturne Press, expressed interest in publishing a hardcover edition of *Moon of the Werewolf,* my novel of Irish werewolves on the rampage in a small Southern town. However, this time, I would be calling the shots and it would be released under the original title, *Undertaker's Moon.* Steven even got an artist friend of his from Texas to do the cover art. That artist was none other than Alex McVey and the cover painting turned out to be his iconic "Blue Werewolf", one of the best and most savage works of lycanthropic horror art brought to visual fruition, in my humble – albeit biased – opinion.

As it turned out, it didn't get published right off the bat. A couple of months afterward, Nocturne folded. After that, Steven started his own press, Croatan Publishing, and fully intended to make UM his first full-length book. He started with a chapbook of my novella, *Flesh Welder,* which had been published by *Noctulpa: Journal of Horror* back in 1990. The cover artist for the book was Zach McCain, another unique and talented artist working out of Texas. Croatan released one more book after *Flesh Welder;* James Newman's short fiction collection, *People are Strange.* After that, the financial burden of keeping a small press afloat became too much for Steven and Croatan ceased to be.

2008 brought about two significant events. First, my son Ryan (aka Bubba) was born. And, secondly, I decided it would be best for me to try my luck at continuing a writing career in mass market publishing, like I had with Zebra; maybe shoot for another chance at writing full-time for a living. At the time, my best bet was Leisure Books, who was publishing horror authors like Brian Keene, Bryan Smith, Edward Lee, Jack Ketchum, Douglas Clegg, and others. I contacted editor Don D'Auria and submitted manuscripts of *Hell Hollow* and *Restless Shadows* to him for consideration for mass market paperback. Both were kindly rejected, which was a blow, since Leisure was the most active and dependable market for paperback horror at the time. Little did I know that Dorchester Publishing would shut down their Leisure Horror line in 2010, leaving dozens of leading authors abruptly without a publisher. It felt like déjà vu. *Here we go again,* I thought, *it's 1996 all over again.*

So, for the time being, I stuck with the independent publishers with really no favorable option to return to the mass market again. As it turned out, the indie presses seemed much more receptive and respectful of my work, possessed a great love of the genre the New York houses definitely lacked, and was interested in the author's creative input concerning cover design, marketing, etc. The indie community felt more like a family or fraternity, than a faceless conglomerate more interested exploiting the author and their talent for the almighty dollar. Back in the 80s and 90s, there had only been a handful of independent presses, namely Dark Harvest and Mark V. Ziesing, while in the latter half of the 2000's there were dozens in operation.

As it turned out, the more I began to submit my work to the indie publishers and immerse myself in that scene, the more it began to feel like home.

My Twelve Favorite RK Mythos Villains & Creatures

1. The Snake Critter | *Fear, Beneath the Branches*
2. Squire Crom McManus aka Arget Bethir | *Undertaker's Moon*
3. Grandpappy Josiah Craven | *Blood Kin*
4. The Thing at the Side of the Road | *The Thing at the Side of the Road*
5. Doctor Augustus Leech | *Hell Hollow*
6. The Snake Queen | *Fear*
7. John Legion | *Strong Steps, The Saga of Dead-Eye*
8. Bully Hanson | *Hindsight, Potter's Field*
9. Evangeline the Witch | *The Saga of Dead-Eye*
10. Mister Glow-Bones | *Mister Glow-Bones, Jingle Bones*
11. Mister Mack | *Mister Mack & the Monster Mobile, Mister Mack is Back in Town*

12. Doctor Nigel Whitehall / *Pretty Little Lanterns*

Chapter Fourteen

Indie Horror Writer

A fter the publication of *Flesh Welder*, the next published work of my 'second' writing career was a novella titled *Tanglewood*. Cemetery Dance published it as a stand-alone chapbook in February of 2008 with a black and white cover by artist Keith Minnion. *Tanglewood* was the first piece of long fiction I wrote after returning to the genre. Some parts in it were a little creaky and awkward, showing that I was a bit rusty after a decade of being away for so long. But there were some creepy imagery and an emotional vein throughout that was encouraging and told me that I was definitely on the right track.

The following year, I had three major victories as far as publications were concerned. Cemetery Dance published a signed hardcover edition of *Midnight Grinding: Tales of Twilight Terror*, my first short story collection The book sported a cover by Alex McVey and was named after a story that had appeared in *Borderlands 3* years before. It was a tale I consider to be one of my most atmospheric and frightening (based on a true incident during my grandmother's childhood as the daughter of an itinerant tobacco farmer in the late 1800s). The book focused on the majority of my published short fiction between 1986 and 1996, and was a solid introduction to my particular brand of Southern horror. CD also included my story "Cumberland Furnace" in Richard Chizmar's *Shivers V* anthology. This one was also based on one of my grandmother's tales... a 'true' ghost story about an actual iron foundry in central Tennessee that used slave labor to manufacture cannonballs for the Confederacy during the Civil War).

It was around this time that I became acquainted with Paul Goblirsch. I had heard through the grapevine that Paul – who lived in Arizona – had started a new independent press called Thunderstorm Books, which specialized in limited editions. I gathered a few of my more extreme, splatterpunk-type stories from the early 90s and put together a small seven tale collection called *The Sick Stuff.* One of the stories was a novelette-length piece titled "Mojo Mama"; a story I had written years ago and had misplaced during my long hiatus. I rewrote it from memory and – in the process – turned it three times more disgusting and disturbing than the original story had been.

I submitted the little collection and Paul accepted it for his Elemental line of digest-sized chapbooks. When Zach McCain ended up doing the cover art for *The Sick Stuff,* I realized that he had embellished my work before with the cover for *Flesh Welder*. Little did I know that, from that point onward, both Zach and Alex would end up doing ninety-percent of my book covers and design work.

Thankfully, *The Sick Stuff* turned out to be a success and solidified a publishing relationship that I've enjoyed with Mr. Goblirsch ever since.

It was toward mid-2009 when I sought out a publisher in hopes of reprinting all of the old Zebra novels in hardcover editions. By then, Kensington had relinquished the rights to *Fear* and *Blood Kin*, so I had the freedom to do with them as I pleased. I made an agreement with Paul Little of Full Moon Books to publish all eight as *The Essential Ronald Kelly Collection.* Unfortunately, as 2009 gave way to 2010, Full Moon published a few public domain horror books such as *Carmilla, Dracula,* and *Frankenstein,* and then promptly went out of business. I began to wonder if maybe I was jinxed and it was my lot in life to doom small press publishers to extinction with each new deal I made.

In August of 2010, Cemetery Dance released the first novel of my comeback. *Hell Hollow* was a coming-of-age tale of four preteens fighting a serial killer possessed by the evil spirit of a traveling medicine show man (and, incidentally, an agent and soul collector of Satan). *HH* also boasted a striking cover by Alex McVey and turned out to be one of my most popular books, garnering several favorable reviews in *Locus* and *Publisher's Weekly.*

Shortly after its publication, I approached Paul at Thunderstorm about the possibility of publishing the *Essential* collection. He jumped at the chance and signed on for all eight books. Alex would do the cover art for the entire series and each book would include a brand new novella related to the characters and storyline of the individual novel. The first of the *Essentials* was the one that had seemed to have a rocky start from the very beginning. *Undertaker's Moon,* Volume 1 in the series, was released in 2011, sporting

Alex's incredible "Blue Werewolf" cover. From that point, the remainder of the *Essential Ronald Kelly Collection* was released, book by book, over the next three years.

Also in 2011, Thunderstorm published my collection of extreme post-apocalyptic horror tales called *After the Burn* as a volume of its Black Voltage series. It contained two novellas and five short stories of a world ravaged by nuclear Armageddon and ruled by murderers, child molesters, and cannibals. At that time I was feeling the pressure of competing with the popular horror authors of that time (Keene, J.F. Gonzalez, James Wrath White, to name a few), and so I pulled out all the stops and wrote some the most intense and extreme fiction of my career. The collection was well-received, but its popularity was short-lived, being only available as a limited edition.

Another book that saw publication in 2011 was my traditional western, *Timber Gray.* Thunderstorm released it as part of its Douglas line of western novels. Simultaneously, Roy Robbins' Bad Moon Books published *Timber Gray*, *After the Burn*, and another story collection, *Cumberland Furnace & Other Fear-Forged Fables* in trade paperback.

It was around this time that I joined forces with David Niall Wilson's Crossroad Press to publish my backlist of novels and collections in e-book and audiobook. Released under the Macabre Ink imprint, my Southern-fried fiction gradually became available through Amazon, Barnes & Noble, Audible, and other digital and audio platforms.

The rest of the *Essential* collection was published by Thunderstorm between 2011 and 2015. In 2014, *Restless Shadows,* the long-awaited sequel to *Hindsight*, was published as a Black Voltage title, along with a short collection of Halloween stories titled *Mister Glow-Bones & Other Halloween Tales* as an Elemental.

So, all in all, it seemed that I was back in full form and publishing regularly with some of the best indie presses in the business. But, unbeknownst to me, things weren't all that they appeared to be. True, I had books coming out, but since the majority were expensive limited editions, it also meant that a limited amount of readers had them gracing their bookshelves.

As 2015 gave way to 2016, I began to slowly realize that I lacked something very essential to my growth and sustainability as a horror author.

Simply put, I lacked an audience.

Grits & Bits

Promoting your work: Once you make the transition from anthology and magazine sales, and begin publishing your own novels, novellas, and collections (and you will with enough effort and persistence), you'll need to let folks know about it. A writer is his/her own best salesperson. The publisher will only do so much in promoting your new release, and some are better at doing it than others. Most independent publishers these days send out ARCs (advanced reading copies) to reviewers and, sometimes, to name authors for a promotional blurb. Some don't, though (due to lack of funds to print ARCs or laziness on their part), and then it is up to you to blow your horn and alert potential readers.

Well, it's sort of tacky and inappropriate to do that, isn't? you might ask. Not really. You have spent a good chunk of your free time and hard work writing, editing, and polishing this book of yours, so you deserve the right to promote it and let folks know it is available. Social media is an excellent tool to get the message out. Twitter, Facebook, Instagram, TikTok; all platforms connect you to the reading public and give you an opportunity to pitch your creation to potential buyers. But, be tasteful about it. Don't post about your new book so much that it seems like you are trying to cram it down their throat. Also, don't proudly herald it as the next best thing in its genre. Confidence is essential, but so is humility.

If your publisher doesn't mail out ARCs, ask them for a mobi eBook file of the book and contact reviewers directly. Many reviewers prefer an eBook file over an actual hands-on book. A good place to start is the book reviewing community on Twitter and the Bookstagram reviewers of Instagram (I have received a lot of positive response from both). Beware of unscrupulous individuals offering to review your book for a fee. I was even approached by one the other day that had a "payment plan" available for his services.

There are other viable ways to promote. Start your own author website, write a blog, and appear on podcasts and You Tube shows to promote your new or upcoming publication and allow potential readers become familiar with you and your work. Author guest readings through genre groups on Goodreads and BookBub promotions can also increase interest and sales.

Chapter Fifteen

Doubt and Disillusion

I came very close to ending my writing career, for good, in 2019. To understand my motivation for even considering such a thing, we need to go back a few years.

2012 and 2013 were emotionally difficult for me and my family. No, difficult doesn't quite cut it. Devastating is more like it. Joyce and I lost six close family members within a short span of eighteen months. It began with my sister-in-law, Debbie, in February of 2012, followed by the deaths of my father in April, Joyce's paternal grandmother in September and her father in November. The next year was no better, with my wife losing another grandmother and a young cousin. The last one was the most heartbreaking of all. Heather had only been 23 years old in the summer of 2013 and had given birth to twins only a few weeks before. Simply put, she laid down for an afternoon nap and never woke up. It turned out that she had suffered from a heart defect that no one had known about, including her or her parents.

As a Christian family, our faith in God carried us through that chain of death and despair, but it was still hard to understand why He would choose to take a mother from her infant children at such a crucial time in their young lives. And the death of my father rocked me to my core. My father and I didn't have an easy relationship. There were times when we were at odds at one another; either he didn't understand me or I didn't understand him. I loved him, there was no doubt about that, but we never enjoyed the easy bond that he and my brother did. A lot of it had to do with us being unable to see eye-to-eye on certain issues. Some of it had to do with my writing; he couldn't understand why I wanted to spend so much time pursuing the dream of being a professional writer or how the hell I expected to make a living at it. We came close to resolving our differences at the end of his life (he even expressed pride in the books I had published), but in 2010 Alzheimer's began to rob him of memory and reason, and, gradually, I became a total stranger to him. After his death, I still found it difficult to find closure. My estranged stepmother cremated him before I had a chance to properly express my love and respect for him. I have absolutely nothing against the practice of cremation, but you must understand something. I came from a traditional Southern family who knew where each and every one of their departed loved ones were buried, from great grandparents on down the line. To not have that grave and headstone to grieve before or be there to pay tribute to as the years passed by was unheard of in our way of thinking. Even now, I have no earthly idea where my father's remains are located. It was like he went missing one day and was never heard from again.

Depression began to set in at the end of 2013 and continued unrelentingly into the following year. Like my mother before me, I had suffered from severe anxiety and depression during my late teens and throughout my twenties. Like before, I found myself avoiding crowds and social gatherings, and began to grow more and more introverted. The thought of eating in a restaurant or attending a party or convention mortified me. And, in turn, it began to affect my writing as well.

In 2014, I began to tease folks in interviews and on podcasts like the late Mark Justice's Pod of Horror about my "Secret Writing Project". In reality, it would be my first original horror novel since the writing of *Restless Shadows* back in 1995. And it would be my first zombie apocalypse novel as well. Zombie literature, as well as AMC's *The Walking Dead* series, was super popular around that time and so I thought it natural to explore that trope for my new novel. But my psyche had different ideas. As I began work on the book, I found that my creativity and motivation was crippled to the point of being null and void (at least in my mind). Depression and anxiety built a formidable wall in my path... a stretch of writer's block that lasted several years. A short 261 page novel that should have only taken a few months to complete turned into a long, four year process.

When *The Buzzard Zone* was finally published by Crossroad Press in 2018, it was not the success that I hoped it would be. In fact, it fell flat on its face. Both interest and sales seemed to be nonexistent. Readers seemed to be indifferent to its publication and so did reviewers. Of course, by then, the zombie craze had run its course and another undead novel (even with a fresh, new twist) was nothing more than white noise to the horror reading public. The lack of response disheartened me and plunged me even further into depression. I had seen a similar reaction (or lack of reaction) to Sinister Grin's paperback release of *Fear, Undertaker's Moon,* and *Hell Hollow* in 2016; it had pretty much been a "Meh!" event. I remember telling Joyce that I was considering hanging it up again... this time once and for all. She urged me to tough it out and not give up; that I'd worked too hard to come back to simply abandon it all over again.

Part of the negativity that gripped me came from social media. I would come across a post on Facebook or Twitter that mentioned me or one of my books and the accompanying comments would include remarks like "Who the hell is he?" or "I've never heard of the guy." I began to come to the realization there was an entire generation of horror readers (maybe even two generations) who had no earthly idea who I was.

Every writer wants to feel that he has left a legacy – a body of work that is enjoyed and respected by readers, not only of his generation, but of future generations. But utter lack of knowledge concerning Ronald Kelly and his backlist of Southern-fried fiction seriously made me wonder if I even had a legacy at all. If the horror-reading public had no earthly idea who I was and was totally unaware of my stories or novels, was continuing to write them even worth the effort? Sadly, I was beginning to think not.

As January of 2019 passed into February, I honestly considering packing up my keyboard and calling it quits. Throughout 2018, I had only made one short story sale; a ghost story titled "Sawmill Road" for *Midnight in the Graveyard*, Ken McKinley's flagship anthology for his new Silver Shamrock Publishing. I knew Ken as a moderator for the Goodreads group Horror Aficionados and he seemed to be genuinely interested in my EC Horror style of Southern-fried fiction. Before I could make the mistake of ending my writing career for the second (and probably final) time, he asked if he could schedule one of my novels for one of HA's monthly group reads. "Which one would you suggest we read?" he asked me, offering me the choice. I didn't have think twice. "I think you should read FEAR."

So, in March 2019, the Horror Aficionados read my seventh Zebra novel, which I personally considered my magnum opus. The book had been available as a Crossroad e-book for years, but with minimal interest or sales. Surprisingly, the Goodreads group read seemed to breathe new life into that old coming-of-age novel. Folks read FEAR and enjoyed it, and vowed to read more of my work. Sales of all my titles began to rise steadily. My followers on Twitter, Facebook, and Instagram doubled in the matter of a couple of months. Suddenly, all thoughts of quitting were placed on the backburner. I began to realized that maybe this horror-writing gig wasn't kaput after all.

Encouraged, I pitched the notion of doing a sequel to my extreme horror collection, *The Sick Stuff,* to Paul at Thunderstorm and he accepted without hesitation. So, that summer *More Sick Stuff* was scheduled for a hardcover edition. But I was aware that only a limited amount of readers would end up reading it, since only hardcore collectors would be willing to shell out the seventy-five dollars for numbered editions. Therefore, I decided to pitch something to Silver Shamrock that I had in mind for a while, in hopes of reaching a wider readership.

The Essential Sick Stuff would be an extreme horror omnibus of sorts. It would include *The Sick Stuff, More Sick Stuff,* and a new mini-collection, *Even Sicker Stuff;* twenty-three stories in all... half being my splatterpunk stories from the early nineties and half brand new tales. Fortunately, Ken at Silver Shamrock was all for it. I also proposed that Alex McVey do the front cover and multiple black and white interior illustrations. Alex and I had been talking about doing such a project together for years and this seemed to be the perfect opportunity.

As 2019 ended and 2020 began, I came to realization that the only way my career would experience a resurgence was if I began to write new fiction, rather than rely solely on my backlist of novels and short fiction, which I had pretty much been doing since my comeback in 2006. I also knew that having my work available in paperback would be beneficial, for those who preferred to have a physical book in their hands, rather than a digital e-book. David Wilson and David Dodd of Crossroad rereleased *Undertaker's Moon* as Volume One of their Resurrected Horrors line and a BookBub promotion shortly afterward propelled *UM* to Number One in Occult Horror for a short time. Sales began to climb and continued with a new paperback release of *The Buzzard Zone*, which sported McVey's original Thunderstorm cover art.

Then, around March of 2020, COVID-19 rose from a few isolated cases to a full-blown pandemic of worldwide proportion. Restaurants, hair salons, and movie theaters closed their doors and folks sequestered themselves in their homes out of fear of contracting the virus. Many writers reacted in different ways to the pandemic; some suffered writer's block or creative apathy, while others found that their creativity had been ignited and set into motion. I was one of the latter. It was like the period of inactivity kicked me in the ass and said, "Take advantage of this free time and get to work!" And, so I did. I had always been a short fiction writer more than a novelist, so I worked on putting together some new story collections for later in the year.

In September of 2020, *The Essential Sick Stuff* was released. It was very well received, earned positive reviews, and was praised by the likes of Brian Keene, Jonathan Janz, and Richard Chizmar. Little did I know that *ESS* would end up winning the Splatterpunk Award for Best Collection a year later.

On the heels of *The Essential Sick Stuff*, Crossroad released *The Halloween Store and Other Tales of All Hallows Eve* in the fall and *Season's Creepings: Tales of Holiday Horror* in December. Both seemed to satisfy readers' desire for nostalgia and comfortable familiarity amid 2020's chaotic uncertainty and it showed in sales and critical praise, particularly among the Bookstagram community on Instagram.

Despite being a lifelong introvert, I began to appear on podcasts such as *Killing Time* and *Dead Headspace* with hosts Patrick McDonough and Brennan LaFaro. My status as a former Zebra Books writer – which had once been a mark of shame in the horror community a couple of decades before – now conjured respect and fascination, rather than ridicule and scorn.

As I settled into a solid writing routine and began to plan more novel releases and short stories for 2021, I realized that patience and tenacity was the key to surviving that ugly bout of doubt and disillusion two years before. If I had given in to self-pity and defeat the way I had intended at the beginning of 2019, folks would have likely seen the end to my particular brand of Southern-fried storytelling. But returning to my first love of the written word – short fiction – saved me from that fate.

And, so, it continues...

TrickorTweet 2021

I n October of 2021, the horror community indulged in an exercise of creativity and writing ability called #trickortweet2021. Using the annoying 280 characters that Twitter has imposed on their "tweets", authors wrote mini horror stories within those boundaries and posted them on social media. Here are some of the ones I came up with:

It dwelled in the dark cellar beneath us. It grew lonely. Came up to be with us in the dead of night. It ate our food, crawled into our beds, and snuggled with us without our knowing. Then it went back down again. But it didn't want to stay there...

"Someone's in Timmy's room."
"No one goes in Timmy's room since..."
The accident. The funeral. The grave with the little stone.

Both walking down the hallway, slowly, like in a dream.
No... a nightmare.
Listening at the door.
"Mommy, Daddy... come see me..."

It flooded all night long. The morning after, when the water had receded, things were found in the roads and yards. One was a boot with a man's foot inside.

The bone had been gnawed and whittled away. Someone had been pulled down, but not by water and mud...

Cindy watches as Daddy circles the bed where Mommy sleeps. The yardstick measures... from her head to her toes, then shoulder to shoulder. Cindy promised him she wouldn't tell. About the special bed. The one like Grandma's metal one, but made of wood and nails.

The old man sat on his porch and watched. The cars driving by. Stray dogs and cats on the sidewalk.

But, most of all, he watched the children. Laughing and playing. Beneath his blanket, he clutched the knife... waiting for them to step one inch onto his lawn.

Chester arrived at the cemetery to find an open grave. Had an animal done it? The Millers' St. Bernard had dug into one once, but not to the very bottom. Then he noticed the broken hinges on the empty casket. The grave had been opened... from the inside out.

The milkshake had tasted a little funny, but she had drunk it all. The frosty treat had looked pinker through the straw... but it *was* strawberry.

Lifting the lid for a peek.

The eyeball stared up at her from the bottom, startled and sad... lost... wondering why.

The woman on the bridge held no substance; no flesh or blood or breath. Only mist and loneliness.

As headlights approached, she would appear. Hoping... praying... that they would turn sharply.

Through the railing, into dark water, where her bloated body awaited.

It came down from the treetops during our picnic in the woods. Snatched Zoe from her playpen and took flight. As I pursued, a vast winged shadow engulfed me... talons sank deep into muscle and bone. It was then that I realized I was chasing a baby carrying a baby.

(Then there was this one from author Vivian R. Kasley, about a diabolical feller in the mountainous wilds of Tennessee:)

Ronald knew the mountains like the back of his hand; the beauty and horrors they held. So, when the leaf peeping hikers, who he'd seen littering just moments before, stopped to ask where they should head next, he smiled, then sent them where the horrors dwell.

(Hmmm... Fear County perhaps?)

Chapter Sixteen

Running the Rabbit

A little over a month ago, I turned sixty-two.

Most men at that age have sobering thoughts in mind. Stuff like mortality, fatality, and a gradual approach toward one's personal "end of days". Declining eyesight, dulled hearing, chronic aches and pains... a mailbox full of AARP and the promise of the exalted "senior discount".

I remember when I first started writing at the tender age of sixteen, I had it all laid out in my mind. "I'll hit it big right after high school, be a best-selling author until I'm in my late fifties or around sixty, then retire." Now here I am a couple years past my imagined retirement age and it simply isn't working out that way. I still have a full-time job (not from writing... that's a part-time gig at best) and still have teenage kids living at home and plenty of bills to pay, just like any other working joe. It's that preconception that Young & Naïve Ron had about retiring the ol' keyboard at sixty that puzzles me the most. Why had I assumed that my creativity and desire to write would be over and done with? I reckon it was just a very young writer's shortsightedness and mistaken belief that creativity would slowly peter out and the ability to pen effective fiction would crash and burn when the candles on my birthday cake grew so plentiful they would trigger a fire alarm.

As it turned out, when I finally got to that point in my 'grand scheme', it wasn't that way at all. Hell... far from it.

We just finished up 2021 and, while we didn't kick Covid's nasty little ass into oblivion like we had hoped, the horror genre was downright robust and unstoppable, like Dr. Banner's gamma green counterpart hopped up on steroids, Viagra, and a twelve-pack of Monster tall-boys. The Big-Five put out their share of New York Times spooky best-sellers, but the majority of the really potent, really innovative fiction originated from the indie presses. Folks like Hailey Piper, Eric Larocca, Laurel Hightower, Samantha Kolesnik, Brennan LaFaro, Janine Pipe, Cynthia Pelayo, V. Castro, and Sonora Taylor, just to name a few. Between novel-length works, novellas, and short stories – both in individual collections and numerous first-rate anthologies – there was certainly no shortage of something exceptional and mind-blowing to read.

I was there, too; busier and more inspired than I had been in years. It started in late-February with a story collection titled *Irish Gothic: Tales of Celtic Horror* from Crossroad Press just in time for St. Patrick's Day, followed by the long-awaited paperback release of my Appalachian vampire novel, *Blood Kin* (which hadn't been available in a hands-on paperback edition since its second printing by Pinnacle Books in 2000.) Later that year, Dawn Shea's D&T Publishing released *The Web of La Sanguinaire & Other Arachnid Horrors*, a collection comprised solely of my spider horror tales.

At the end of that July, I appeared at Scares That Care in Williamsburg, Virginia as a guest author. Believe me, I was more than a little nervous and apprehensive, since it was the first convention I had attended in thirteen years. Fortunately, it turned out to be a fun and wonderful experience. I got to hang out with my old pal, Brian Keene, as well as other authors and publishers I had only interacted with through social media; fine folks like Jonathan Janz, Todd Keisling, Ken McKinley, Kenneth Cain, Patrick McDonough, Wesley Southard, Jeff Strand, Hunter Shea, Kelli Owen, Kevin Lucia, and Sonora Taylor.

In October, Crossroad released a paperback edition of my 2014 collection, *Mister Glow-Bones & Other Halloween Tales*, with cover and interior art by myself. The long-suppressed artist in me finally slipped the chains and broke out the pencils, pen, and ink (which has been satisfying enough to prompt me to plan more illustrated collections in the years to come).

Also, it was the year that Ol' Dead-Eye finally escaped the dusty casket of unfulfilled projects and got his chance to ride, forty-five years after his initial creation. Paul Goblirsch and I had been talking about doing Dead-Eye several years earlier, but the time didn't seem right for either one of us. After the success of Death's Head Press' Splatter Western line, I figured it was as good time as any to saddle Dead-Eye's literary horse and let him ride. As I developed the idea for the series, I decided to refrain from making Dead-Eye a loner and give him a partner on his quest for vengeance and justice. The black Louisiana mojo man, Job, seemed just the right fit and an ample foil for some humorous banter between the two, similar in spirited comradery to Lansdale's Hap and Leonard. I also gave the vampire Jules Holland a trio of evil minions (Snake, Boar, & Rooster), and a dark witch named Evangeline, who had the power to open otherworldly portals and conjure all manner of creatures to do her bidding, including the demonic bounty hunter John Legion (which first made his appearance in my novella "Strong Steps" back in 2016).

At the end of 2021, Thunderstorm Books released the limited hardcover edition of the first entry in the series, THE SAGA OF DEAD-EYE, BOOK ONE: VAMPIRES, ZOMBIES, & MOJO MEN, while Silver Shamrock Publishing released the e-book, paperback, and an affordable hardcover. The following four volumes will be published every six months over the next two years, with the next installment being BOOK TWO: WEREWOLVES, SWAMP CRITTERS, & HELLACIOUS HAINTS. With the unfortunate demise of Silver Shamrock, Crossroad Press stepped in to act as *Dead-Eye*'s publisher. They also took on the publishing of my three volume homage to the EC Horror comics of the 1950s, beginning with HAUNT OF SOUTHERN-FRIED FEAR. The series explores different horror genre themes – the first being ghosts – and future volumes will include TALES FROM THE SOUTHERN-FRIED CRYPT (scary swamp tales), and VAULT OF SOUTHERN-FRIED HORROR (maniacs, serial killers, and murderers).

Now here we are at 2022. As Covid spikes yet once again with the dastardly Omicron, the year continues to promise uncertainty and unease. But we who write the dark stuff labor onward, weaving our own fears and insecurities into tales of terror for the bookshelves of those who revel in such things.

And of what of Ol' Ron? Don't worry. I'm planning on sticking around for a while longer. At this point in my career, I have more irons in the fire than ever before. More volumes of Dead-Eye, more Southern-fried tales with an EC Horror flavor, upcoming collaborations with some storytellers you might know, an illustrated edition of *After the Burn,* and, hopefully, the sequel to *Fear* not too far away.

Some old dogs get tired and lazy when they reach their later years. They choose to lay in the shade of the front porch, to snooze and rest their weary bones... to dream of better days. And, who am I to deny that of them; most deserve it. But for this old hound, the better days are yet to come. He has no time to laze about and reflect on the past.

No, he still has his fair share of rabbits to run.

The Essays

The following essays concerning writing and creating horror fiction previously appeared on my Blogspot, *Southern-Fried & Horrified,* as well as guest blogs on other social media platforms and various publications.

SADDLES, SIX-SHOOTERS, & SEX

You may not be aware of it, but novels of Southern horror weren't the only books I wrote in the early 1990s. I also wrote western novels... albeit under a different name. A very famous name as far as long-running western series were concerned.

Yes, I wrote two novels for the Jake Logan series. That seemingly un-ending line of adult westerns that featured the adventures of John Slocum, an ex-Confederate soldier turned drifter, gambler, lawman, outlaw, cowboy, and about any other occupation that folks in the Old West took up in those bygone days. It was also one of the first series -- along with Longarm, Lone Star, The Gunsmith, and Edge -- that incorporated a healthy dose of hot, steamy sex into its adventurous storylines.

And how did a young author, just starting out in the business, net such a writing coup? Well, pour yourself a

191

shot of rotgut, light up a Clint Eastwood cheroot, and I'll give you the lowdown.

In 1992, around the time that *Moon of the Werewolf (Undertaker's Moon)* was published by Zebra Books, my agent at the time, Joshua Bilmes of the Scott Meredith Agency, called and asked if I would consider filling a lucrative writing spot that had suddenly opened up. When I asked him which one, he said Jake Logan. Now, I had only heard of the series and seen them on about every bookstore rack imaginable, but had never actually read one. I must admit, I was a tad hesitant to answer with a resounding "Hell, yeah!" You see, I was like most young authors back then and one thing I had equal portions of were pride and a bit of an overblown ego.- *What?* I thought, *"write a book that won't be published under MY name!"* The thought of ghost-writing at the time was almost taboo in the back of my mind. After all, the main reason I wrote under my natural moniker of Ronald Kelly -- and balked at the thought of using a pen name like some of my contemporaries -- was because I felt I had something to prove. A high school creative writing teacher -- upon learning that had no plans to attend college -- shook her head in patronizing pity. "No one becomes a published author without a college education," she said, as if giving a grim and gloomy eulogy at a funeral of my own making. But, coming from a rural family where folks barely graduated high school, let alone even contemplated college, I followed family tradition and got a full-time job in the factories, while attempting to forge a writing career on the side. It took twelve long years of honing my writing skills through trial and error, and submitting endless reams of short stories and articles without success, before I finally began selling horror stories to small press horror magazines in the mid-80s; publications like *Deathrealm, Grue, Noctulpa*, and, of course, Rich Chizmar's *Cemetery Dance*.

Anyway, I told my agent that I would consider it and would let him know something within a week or two. He told me not to wait very long. Apparently, Jake Logan had a small stable of ghost writers, four or five at the most, and the one I was to replace had, sadly, kicked the bucket. If I didn't jump into the empty spot soon, it would go to another writer.

I wrestled with the idea for a few days, then decided to call someone who had been in the publishing business a while longer than I had. The someone I called for advice was none other than Joe R. Lansdale, hisownself. Now, I had known Joe for a while; we'd traded correspondence and talked over the phone from time to time (that's what we did back yonder before the internet made things a hell of a lot easier), and a year earlier he had accepted my dark Louisiana Cajun story "Beneath Black Bayou" for *Dark at Heart*, a crime/suspense/horror anthology that he and his wife, Karen, had put together for Dark Harvest. So I called him up one evening and caught him just as he was leaving for martial arts training (I seemed to be annoying like that, in an eager puppy-dog kind of way). As usual, Joe was gracious to the max (sounding a lot like a Nacogdoches, Texas version of Charlie Daniels). When I asked him about ghost-writing, he admitted that he had done it before, as well as having written under a pen name, and that it was no big deal. I thanked him and called my agent back the next day. And started my brief (*very* brief) gig as a genuine western ghost-writer

The first thing I received from Berkley Books was a contract and the Jake Logan Bible. The contract stipulated that for each Jake Logan western I wrote, I would earn a flat $5,000 with no royalties to be paid out afterwards. In my mind that was fair trade; five-Gs for a measly 180 page book seemed like a godsend at that time in my writing career. Despite the fact that I was writing regularly for Zebra, times were tough. My wife, Joyce, and I would pick up cans by the side of the road and cash them in for supper money... which usually consisted of a 24 count box of fish sticks and a box of cheap macaroni and cheese (the powdered kind, not the deluxe stuff with the real cheese packet).

The Jake Logan Bible consisted of fifty double-spaced pages stapled together and told you everything you wanted to know about writing for the series. It gave the background and history of the hero, John Slocum, as well as popular plot examples and writing tips. It also gave, in great and steamy detail, the particulars of writing the customary three to four sex scenes that were required for each novel. Lordy Mercy, it was almost as good as a copy of Penthouse! It gave various sexual positions and places where Slocum and that novel's western hottie could perform the dirty deed. At the side of the trail, in a saloon's upstairs room, in the rocking chair on the front porch of a lonely widows farmhouse... the choices were endless. It also told you what Slocum was allowed -- and not allowed -- to do, during his sexual escapades. Ol' John was open to any position imaginable, but there was some things he wouldn't engage in. Oral sex (as foreplay) was okay, but under no circumstances would there be any type of anal sex. Slocum didn't plow the mudhole, no matter how horny he might be. And there would be no taboo stuff, like bestiality (which happened with sheep and such a lot back then). Slocum could dally around with the heroine-of-the-month, but his horse stayed in the barn, safe and unmolested, where it belonged.

So, in 1993 and 1994, I wrote and published two Jake Logan westerns. *Slocum and the Nightriders* (#174) was about the hero getting caught in the middle of a range war between a poor rancher and a dastardly cattle baron. *Slocum and the Gold Slaves (#187)* took a departure from the usual western setting, having Slocum drugged and abducted during a whorehouse tryst and ending up in a glory-hole in Alaska, digging for gold with a team of similarly shanghaied prisoners. I must admit, figuring out the three sex scenes for *Gold Slaves* - was a bit tricky. Slocum is abducted immediately after a whore-hopping scene and ends up slinging a pick in the frigid depths of the gold mind. So how in the world is he going to get lucky, in a mine full of men, with nary a frolicsome harlot in a five hundred mile radius? That's where Blake Duboise entered the picture; a stage actress who masqueraded as a man to locate her father, a prospector that owned the Glory Hole, but had mysteriously disappeared. After being captured, she was subjected to manual labor, before her true gender was discovered by Slocum. Believe you me... it took some nimble acrobatics on their part to get it on amongst ice cold boulders with their ankles chained securely together. But where there's a will, there's a way, I reckon.

One other thing that I included in both Jake Logan novels, was my last name somewhere in the storyline (that youthful pride rearing its ugly head again). In *Nightriders* it was rancher George Kelly and his voluptuous nymphomaniac of a daughter, Prissy. While in *Gold Slaves* the one who abducted John Slocum and spirited him away to the Glory Hole was none other than the legendary slave-trader Shanghai Kelly himself.

It took me a mere two weeks to complete each novel and, afterward, I collected a cool five-grand for each. I began brainstorming further Slocum adventures, figuring I was going to turn that gig into a lucrative side career... and, in the process, start eating sirloin steak instead of Raman noodles. Then, suddenly and most unexpectedly, it all came to a halt. Berkley decided to end the Jake Logan series for an indefinite period of time. Discouraged, I went back to my horror writing and left the adult-western genre behind. Six months later, they decided to bring Jake Logan back, but despite my intentions to return to the series they had already hired another writer to fill the vacant spot, leaving me out of the picture.

I reckon I can't complain. I earned ten grand out of the gig, as well some much-need writing experience and some valuable lessons in big name mid-list publishing and contract clauses and stipulations. Wikipedia has me listed as one of the Jake Logan writers and you can find-*Nightriders* and *Gold Slaves* in used bookstores and listed on eBay every now and then.

So, if you like your western adventures with a little raunchy action peppered throughout the cliff-hanger chapters, you might want to search out the two I had the opportunity... and, yes, *pleasure..* to pen. And if you want to sit, naked, in your armchair late at night, wearing only boots, chaps, and a Stetson, flipping feverishly to the naughty parts... well, more power to you, partner.

Prose Mechanics Evolution!

A random comment or two on a Twitter post a few days ago led Sadie Hartmann (known by those of us who love and cherish her as Mother Horror) to ask me to elaborate on the way writers have performed the physical process of turning prose into the printed word over the years. In my case, it has been 45 years since the writing bug first bit me – rather hard – at the age of 15.

Not to sound like some grizzled, old dog horror writer (which, truthfully, I am), but today's writers just don't realize how easy they have it. I'm not talking about the creative process itself; that's always been hard work, along with developing technique and finding your own distinct voice. What I'm referring to is the actual *physical* way we write and submit our work for publication. A lot of young writers have only known the current and modern way; writing on a computer and then, after editing and polishing, saving it digitally and emailing it off to potential editors and publishers. But for those of us who have been doing this for a while – and by a while, I mean twenty years or more – the physical act of writing has evolved over the years, from methods that are now considered crude and unproductive to the high-tech, internet-driven processes we have readily available today.

This is my story... how the act of writing and submitting work changed, quite dramatically, within a span of nearly fifty years.

1976

Midway through the 1970s, during my senior year in high school, I made the decision to abandon a longstanding desire to be a comic book artist and focus solely on writing short stories and novels. I was young, naïve, and full of lofty dreams of being the next Stephen King. As my junior year stretched into my senior year, I began to commit my ideas to paper, mostly college-ruled notebooks and legal pads. This was not a bad way to start out writing and I know professional authors today who still pen their first rough draft in longhand, before taking it to the next level. There is a definite advantage to committing your thoughts and ideas to paper through the physical act of longhand, especially if your inspiration is coming at a fast and frenetic pace.

1977

Of course, after a while, you had the desire to actually see your work typed out in neat, uniform rows, much as it would be on the printed page of the book. It was then that you would crave ownership of the magical word machine known as a typewriter. I'm certain there were probably electric typewriters in 1977, but they were mostly for office or corporate use and were incredibly expensive. So, most students and novice writers had to depend on the manual version. My first manual typewriter was a fossil; an old 1920 Underwood Number 5. You know the kind; the ones you see newspaper reporters use in all those black and white 30s and 40s movies. Tall, industrially aesthetic, and heavy as lead at a solid 40 pounds, the Underwood Number 5 only came in the color black, the same as Henry Ford's Model-T. The one I had come from a storage room of the tool and die company my father worked at, after the front office had been updated to more modern machinery. To say that it was intimidating to sit before is practically an understatement. I always felt like some lowly, unworthy sinner standing before some dark and somber cathedral. Given that the typewriter was nearly sixty years old, it had its share of quirks and problems. Changing the ink-infused cotton ribbon was like threading an old-time movie projector and the long type arms tended to bind and stick, especially on the A, E, and I... the most commonly-used letters in the English language. Also, the letters tended to either smear or imprint lightly on the paper you were typing on, causing the text on the page to appear unappealing and sometimes downright illegible.

When I was seventeen, my parents got me another manual typewriter for Christmas. It wasn't brand new; precision typing equipment was still expensive then, especially for families of limited income such as mine. They bought mine second-hand through a classified ad in the newspaper. It was a 1955 Royal Quiet Deluxe and it was a creamy pink in color. My dad wasn't very keen on his son having a *pink* typewriter, but I was just glad to have a decent one that worked smoothly with no contrary keys to slow me down (I've since discovered that, as far as the Quiet Deluxe was concerned, pink was the most popular color that it came in). The ribbon changed easier than the old Underwood. It still wound from spool to spool, from one side to the other, and most ribbons were two-toned, with black on the top and red on the bottom, with a switch built into the typewriter to switch from one color to the other. It was on this typewriter that I typed my first short stories and, eventually, a couple of novels that never saw publication. I was just testing the waters at that time, getting the feel of turning my thoughts and ideas into credible, saleable prose.

1982

After graduating high school and entering the workforce, I struggled with the little pink Royal for a while, then got the hankering to indulge in more modern technology. Electric typewriters were becoming more and more affordable, and a personal home model would run you between two hundred and fifty to three hundred dollars in the early 80s. Having my own money to invest in a new machine, I chose the Smith Corona SL 400. It was a smooth piece of technology with automatic return (instead of having to manual shift the roller carriage yourself) and a clever revolving type of wheel that you could interchange for different fonts. It was on this typewriter that I wrote the first few novels that I submitted to several New York literary agents, including the Scott Meredith Agency, which represented me during my years with Zebra Books.

This is the point in the narrative where I should tell you exactly what an aspiring or professional writer had to endure at that time. First, you would type a rough draft of a story or novel, then a second version, painstakingly correcting and editing as you went. That involved many realms of typing paper and ribbon cartridges. After a presentable copy was completed, you would go to the local library to have it photocopied or find someone who worked somewhere that had a business copier. Home copiers were pretty much out of the question in the early 80s. They were too expensive and so were the cartridges that they went through at an annoying fast rate. These days, you can run out to Walmart and buy a good copier that copies, scans, and faxes for fifty bucks or under. Back then, one that simply copied could cost you five hundred bucks or more.

Anyway, after the copying, there was the submission process. When I started submitting short stories to small press horror magazines like *Cemetery Dance-, Deathrealm, Eldritch Tales* and *Grue*, you kept a physical copy for yourself and mailed the other to the publisher with a self-addressed, stamped envelope. Then you waited. Sometimes you didn't hear anything for three to nine months, sometimes a year or more. But you didn't agonize over it. You just kept on writing and submitting, hoping something would catch an editor's eye and net you a sale. There was no internet to speak of at that time, so everything was done via snail mail and that's how the process pretty much remained until the year 2000 or so.

The Smith Corona SL 400 served me well, but when it finally went on the blink in 1987 due to a bad circuit board, it turned out to be a real pain in the ass. The writing of my first certified horror novel, *Hindsight*, was put on hold for three months while my typewriter languished on a dusty shelf at the local Smith Corona repair shop, awaiting a replacement for the defective part. I often wonder if it were fickle Fate taking a hand in the grand scheme of things and if the novel would have even been accepted by Kensington Publishing if the timeline had proceeded differently. I guess we'll never really know.

1990

At the end of the 80s, I had finally reached a lifelong goal and was officially a professional, published author. Dozens of my stories had appeared in leading small press magazines and anthologies, and mass market publisher Kensington had bought two novels for their

Zebra Books horror line. After finishing the second book, *Pitfall*, I proceeded to the next step in cutting edge writing technology: the word processor. The word processor was mainly an electric typewriter with a monitor and a hard drive with which to save your work on floppy disk. You could also edit, polish, and delete during the writing process, which saved you a small fortune in correction tape and Liquid Paper. After your story was saved and ready, you merely pressed a button and the typewriter would act as a printer, delivering a slick, pristine copy of your work. I chose the Smith Corona PWP System 14. The setup was easy to work with, but its black screen with stark green text would absolutely kill your eyes after sitting there for hours at a time.

1993

I had been publishing books with Zebra for three years before I finally decided to buy a personal computer. The physical process of writing, printing, and submitting work by mail was as it always had been. The internet was still in its infancy and email hadn't yet been implemented as a viable way to transmit your literary files to agents or publishers. So, where did I go to get my first PC? Why, good ol' Radio Shack, of course. The Tandy 1000 was the one I chose and I ended up writing novels like *Fear, Blood Kin,* and *Hell Hollow* on it. Being a computer novice, I had no idea that the system was outdated and basically obsolete in the rapidly-evolving PC market. It had limited storage space and Radio Shack retired the model in 1994. I put my Model 1000 to good use until 1996.

2006

This is the point in the story where you say "Whoa! Didn't you just say that you used that last PC until 1996? So, why did you wait so long to buy another one?"

That's because, in October of 1996, Kensington uninceremoniously shut down the Zebra Horror line and I was abruptly without a job. So I stopped writing, period, for ten long years. Part of my decision was due to my frustration at having lost my publishing career and my inability to find another publisher who was willing to publish horror after the devastating Horror Implosion of the mid-Nineties. The other part was my sincere belief, as a Christian, that God had had a hand in ending my writing career because He simply didn't want me writing the stuff. I no longer believe that way, but I did back then.

So, when I finally decided to come back to the horror genre in 2006 (after the encouragement of fans and friends), I discovered that the ways of writing and submitting had changed quite a bit. Sending your work off via the United Postal System was pretty much a thing of the past. Manuscripts were transmitted to editors and publishers through email, much the way Scotty beams Kirk, Spock, and the poor, doomed Red Shirts to the planet's surface during an away mission.

To tell the truth, I was completely ignorant of the new process and had to scramble to update my knowledge of the publishing industry and the tools with which to best compete in it. A week or so after I decided to launch my comeback, I went to BestBuy and bought an HP Pavilion Media Center TV M7470n Desktop.

The HP M7470 served me well in the years to come. I began to submit new work and edit and prepare the old Zebra novels for republication as the Essential Ronald Kelly Collection, which Thunderstorm Books released in limited edition hardcovers between 2011 and 2015. Through the years since, I've stuck with the HP brand because that seems to be what suits my needs the best.

There you have it. My own personal experience with the gradual evolution of writing technology from 1975 to present day. So, when I scroll through posts on Facebook or Twitter and see today's writers gripe and complain about how hard it is to write and submit their work, please forgive me if I smile and shake my head... and remember what I and other authors of my era had to go through to get our stories and books written, submitted, and published.

Walking the Fence Rail: Balancing Faith and Horror Writing

W hen I was a young boy, I would walk the fence on Grandpa Kelly's farm. On one side there would be green grass and soft clover; on the other, thistle and blackberry bramble, with plenty of sharp rocks hidden underneath. It wouldn't have taken much at all to have lost my balance and fallen one way or the other, but I never did. Mostly it was due to my own youthful balancing act, but sometimes it was because Grandpa held my hand while I walked the rail.

Often, that's how it feels when it comes to my faith and my horror writing career. On one side there is all goodness and light, while on the other there are sharp thorns, dangerous shadows, and the potential for a disastrous fall. You may think it is an unlikely and incompatible combination that was doomed to failure from the beginning. But you would be wrong. There are more Christian horror writers out there than you would think. I've talked to quite a few and, amid our discussions, found that we all hold the same doubts and fears. We definitely have questions about what we're doing from time to time. Some of them are of our own making, while others come from fans or members of our spiritual niche. The following are some issues that we are forced to address -- for ourselves as well as for others -- every now and then.

Am I compromising my faith by choosing to write this particular genre of fiction? No, I don't think so. As a Christian, I believe that God has a hand in all aspects of my life, both personal and professional, and that includes my talent and desire to write. I developed a strong interest in monsters and the macabre at an early age (one that my mother shared and reinforced) so you might say that I was "predestined" to write and create this sort of stuff later in life. Believe me, I've tried my best to specialize in other genres over the years; science fiction, mystery, western, children's literature, even inspirational. But horror was the only one I was actually successful (or happy) with. I'm relatively good at it, seem to know how to press readers' emotional buttons, and I have something of a warped and dark sense of humor. I see this as more of a blessing than a fluke or coincidence. People are always referring to someone's "God-given talent" in an off-hand way, but I believe there is more truth to that than folks realize.

Is it sinful to write horror fiction? Whenever someone asks me this question, I can't help but think of a hundred cartoons I've seen in my lifetime: the well-meaning guy with an angel perched on one shoulder and a devil on the other, persuading him to do either right or wrong. I don't know about other horror authors, but that isn't how it is with me. For the most part, I don't feel conflicted while writing horror fiction; it seems to flow naturally, with no mental shifting between "good and bad" taking place. Sure, there are some instances when I feel like I've stepped past my comfort zone, but that's what gives horror its edge... the author's willingness to go a step further and take the reader into realms they would, in life, hesitate to tread. As for the horror genre being evil? Only those who don't read it or aren't familiar with it seem to hold that opinion. I've actually had several people -- some of them family members -- call me a "devil worshiper" because I write this stuff. There's a misconception among a small minority of people (mostly radical religious groups) that writers and film directors of horror-related material are actually in league with the Devil. Of course, thinking in such a way is both ignorant and preposterous. I've met hundreds of horror authors since I began writing in the genre in 1986 and 99% of them were some of the nicest and most wholesome people I've ever met. Some have been fellow Christians, some atheists and agnostics, some straight, some gay... which proves what a diverse body of wordsmiths the horror genre boasts compared to, say, the romance and western genres.

Do you inject your religious beliefs into your stories and novels? No, not consciously. I consider my faith a personal matter and prefer not to inject it into my fiction, lest it be considered as "preachy". Besides, trying to fuse religion with horror (as in "Christian horror", a strange and seemingly contrary sub-genre to be sure) very rarely works. It's like mixing oil with water. Sometimes religious themes, characters, or settings surface in my books, but I'm not sure if I've done it with the intention of actually sharing my faith. After the Burn had a definite undercurrent of religion throughout and, I suppose, the last story in the collection, "The Paradise Pill", even gave the reader a glimpse of a heaven which may or may not be. The mass murder from my novel Father's Little Helper (currently available under its original title *Twelve Gauge)* took place in a country church at Christmas time, and of course Grandpappy Craven from Blood Kin had been a mountain preacher before vampirism caused him to trade his Bible and cross for a hankering for blood. So, perhaps, subconsciously, I do let my faith show through a little in plots and characters.

Am I expressing a hidden side of myself when I write about evil or ungodly characters? This is where a lot of writers of horror fiction experience the most friction. When family, co-workers, or even members of one's church, discover that they write "those awful horror stories", then perceptions begin to alter and the author is suddenly regarded in a different, less favorable light. Most "regular" folks (and by that I mean those who don't possess a love for the macabre) believe that surely something must be mentally or morally wrong with someone who would write about monsters or serial killers and, in turn, derive pleasure from doing it. Writing horror doesn't make you an unstable person, a devil worshipper (there's that enigma again), a weirdo, or a child molester. As I said before, most of the time it's the normal folks who specialize in the horror, suspense, and mystery fields... and I could add science-fiction and fantasy to that grouping as well. To tell the truth, it would be the full-blown romance writer, especially the ones who fill their books with ultra-explicit sex and wanton debauchery who I would be wondering about. Actually, there are some Christians (and I've been told this myself by fellow believers) who think that is morally wrong to write about vampires, werewolves, demons, zombies, and ghosts because they are of "Satan's dominion" and it is sinful to "glorify" such creatures. I, myself, don't believe that such monsters exist, maybe with the exception of demons, whose presence is apparent every day in countless news stories about terrorists, child murderers, and those who commit crimes too horrible to even comprehend. Writing about evil characters (the antagonist) or terrible, unthinkable situations or plot twists, doesn't mean that your Dr. Jekyll is unleashing its Mr. Hyde. A person can write about both good and evil without actually being one or the other; that's the gift of a good writer... they can wear many hats convincingly. Being a horror writer no more makes you a carbon copy of your most fiendish character than wearing mouse ears makes you Mickey Mouse or sporting a dab of a mustache on your upper lip makes you Adolf Hitler. Prose is a creative action, like painting or playing music. If a writer's story is about an axe murderer, that doesn't mean he or she is going to take up a hatchet and chase you gleefully around your front lawn. It is simply an exercise in imagination that takes a darker path than other genres take.

Why would God approve of or even want you to write horror fiction? This is the number one question that horror writers of the Christian faith ask themselves from time to time. The very nature of being a person of faith is to question things that do not involve goodness and benevolence. Philippians 4:8 says "Finally, brethren, whatsoever things are true, whatsoever things are honest, whatsoever things are just, whatsoever things are pure, whatsoever things are lovely, whatsoever things are of good report, if there be any virtue, and if there by any praise, think on these things." Basically, that means almost everything that horror is not. Truthfully, I believe in everything in the Bible, from Genesis to Revelations. But I've always had an aversion to Philippians 4:8, simply because it condemns a person's interest in things dark and mysterious, which is not only a major pastime of mine, but, frankly, my bread and butter. I've actually had fellow Christians throw this scripture in my face when I suggested that they read one of my novels or stories.

I had a huge problem with this question following the implosion of the Zebra horror line back in 1996 and the sudden loss of my first career as a novelist. Having recently "found religion", as the old-timers call it, I became convinced that God had taken away my writing career because He didn't want me to write horror. That might sound silly to you, but to a believer, whose faith dictates that God is instrumental in all things, it is practically logical. So I gave it up... for ten years. It was a long journey of self-doubt and denial, and it took a long time for me to realize that I was downright miserable because of my self-imposed hiatus. It was only when I returned to the genre in 2006, that I was truly happy creatively again. I originally intended to tone my tales down considerably, but discovered that you simply couldn't do that with horror fiction. True, I'm not as "in-your-face" as other horror authors, but I do use a little profanity (never the F-bomb or the Lord's name in vain) and include occasional sexual situations; I just don't go overboard for the sake of offending or grossing my readership out.

If the Lord has a purpose for my writing this stuff, I'd have to say it would be the perpetuation of "good versus evil" storytelling. There was a time in horror literature (any literature, to tell the truth) when the good guys always won and the bad guys got their just dues. These days, fiction isn't as black and white as it once was. More often than not, it is a battle between evil and a lesser or greater evil. I reckon I'm just old-school, because this approach irks me a lot. In my way of thinking, if you don't have a clear-cut protagonist and antagonist, then it is simply not horror fiction... or at least not the kind that I enjoy and write.

In the horror genre, there are all kinds. I just happen to be one of the choir boys of the bunch. If you don't agree with what I've said, remember, this is simply my opinion and how I feel concerning these particular questions. You may believe or disbelieve; that's your God-given right. As for me, I definitely believe that there is something more than talent and luck involved in the success of my writing career and I know precisely who to give all the glory to for that. And if I need a Fatherly hand to keep me balanced on the literary fence rail, then I'll gladly hold onto it.

A Word from the Pulp-Writing, Zebra-Striped, Retro-90s Horror Hack

R ecently, I've been reading some fan reviews of my novels on Goodreads and other online websites, and I've come to a sobering realization. For the most part, folks enjoy my work... but they don't take it very seriously.

Does this bother me? Maybe a little. I suppose every writer starts out a new novel or short story putting everything they have into it and hoping that their work will gain respect and touch someone in a creative and emotional way. But I reckon when it comes down to pleasing horror fans and critics, you can either go in one of two directions. Do you want to be a serious, high-browed author of the macabre or an old-fashioned writer of pulp horror and spooky tall-tales? Do you want to impress readers with your English degree and wow them with your intellectual prose... or do you simply want to have some fun and tell a good story?

According to the majority of those who've read my brand of Southern-fried horror, I fit into the latter category.

From a review of my novel, Fear, J.B. says: Every so often, I crave something dumb in my entertainment diet. Not dumb like a Michael Bay movie or "Twilight" or network TV. I said dumb, not worthless. I mean something creatively dumb. Something that lets me give my mind a rest but that doesn't insult my intelligence. I mean dumb as in an all-night flying saucer movie marathon, an old-school Mack Bolan, or meathead metal. I mean dumb as in early '90s cheap horror paperbacks.

Dumb? This worried me a bit. Is this fella saying that my books are dumb? Worse, is he saying that I'm dumb? That old Irish temper of mine wasn't quite at a boil, but it was starting a slow simmer. Then I continued reading...

About 15 or 20 years ago, publishing outfits such as Zebra, Leisure, and Pinnacle were the kings of supermarket book racks, carpet-bombing their aisles with goofy vampires, werewolves, demon children, etc. who glared with glowing eyes off foil, cut-out covers that tore nanoseconds after purchase. I bought armloads of the things, along with a big bag of picante Cornquistos (greatest snack food EVAH!) to go along with the junk food prose. Among the better purveyors of this kind of pulp was Ronald Kelly, the Zebra poor man's version of Joe Lansdale.

Okay, I'll agree with that. The guy knows of what he speaks. Mass market paperback houses such as Pinnacle and Zebra (of which I was sort of an indentured servant of the literary type) did over-saturate the book racks with horror novels, both good and bad, and around the mid-90s, caused an implosion that knocked quite a few writers off their feet and out of a job... me included. That I was considered to be one of the "better purveyors" of paperback horror during that period is a compliment and anytime I'm compared to Joe Lansdale in any manner, positive or negative, it is a good thing in my book.

Most Zebra writers didn't require a repeat visit. A lot of the books that publisher put out were just plain garbage and contributed to the sinking of the horror market a few years later. Turns out that saturating the shelves with crap was not a good long-term business strategy. But I liked Kelly's books. They were unpretentious, solidly constructed, meat 'n' taters, good 'n' evil horror stories. Kelly isn't likely to win any prizes for his glittering sentences or his eye-opening insight into the nature of man, but he knows how to tell a story. Too damn many "serious" authors haven't clue No. 1 about the mechanics of plot. I bought all the Kelly books and stashed em away until I'd get my next craving for good dumb popcorn fun.

This is where the unshakable stigma of being a "Zebra Hack" comes in. Even before the Big Z accepted my first novel, Hindsight, for publication in 1989, they had a shoddy reputation. For two years my agent submitted the book to almost every paperback house in New York City and, after running the course from A to Z, it was finally accepted at Zebra. The acceptance was bittersweet. I was overjoyed to finally have a publisher, but not so happy that it was Zebra. During the first leg of my horror writing career (I'm currently on the second one) I always felt like horror aficionados and my horror-writing peers regarded me as second-string (or less) because I wrote for Zebra. At the first World Horror Convention, I even had Charles Grant ask me

215

point-blank "Why the hell are you tied up with Zebra? You could do so much better than them!"

I reckon it just comes down to this: everyone has to start out somewhere. You do as well as you can with what you have at that particular point in time... and at that point in my wet-behind-the-ears writing career, my only chance at mass market publication was the dreaded Z. So I stuck with them and tried to buck the traditional Zebra formula. Instead of writing five or six evil child/doll novels in a row, I wrote something different every time. And I fought to retain my Southern identity, even though the folks at Zebra accused me of being too "rural" more times than I could shake a stick at. I wrote 8 books under the Zebra imprint before the bottom dropped out and they shut down their horror line. I always did my best to be a cut-above the average Zebra author (the way the late, great Rick Hautala did) and, according to this particular review, I managed to accomplish that.

J.B. makes another good point here, too. When it all comes down to it, it's all about "telling the story". You can have the most brilliant plot in the history of literary fiction, but if you don't know how to tell the story -- how to invent characters that you genuinely care about and develop situations that are reasonably credible and fun to read -- then your book will have no soul and it will fall flat on its face. I've read a number of books since coming back to the horror genre in 2006 and, for the most part, they were good, solid stories. But more than a few had all the pizzazz and appeal of a technical manual for a toaster, Whenever someone reviews one of my books and uses the term "throwback to the pulp paperback days of the '80s and '90s horror boom", I take it as a compliment. Because that was when the genre was at its pinnacle, in my opinion. That was when everyone involved had an individual voice and style, from Stephen King himself to the lowliest horror hack. And no one seemed to be particularly concerned about sales or popularity. Most of us were just having too much dadblamed fun to care.

In another review, L.W. says: If Stephen King's fiction, by his own admission, is the equivalent of a Big Mac and fries, then Kelly's is most certainly an RC Cola and a Moon Pie.

This classification of "junk food literature" in comparison to, say, "steak & lobster literature" seems to be a recurring theme here. If King is part of that common-man fraternity, then so am I. If fast-paced, adventurous fiction that leans more toward fun and fright than grim intellectualism and unsettling dread, is your cup of tea (or sweet tea, in my case), then I'm your man.

More than likely, I won't ever win any major awards for my down-home horror (as of yet, the Stoker folks have neglected to bless me with one of those spooky, little outhouses), but I really don't care. The reward is writing what I want, how I want, and having readers derive some enjoyment from the end result. And, if I accomplish that by using shivers and smiles, then I can punch the ol' literary time clock and feel good about it at the end of the day.

Where Are the Children?:The Decline of the Coming-of-Age Novel

When my novel Hell Hollow was published in 2009, more than one reviewer (several in fact) said something to this effect: "Kelly's newest novel, which has a group of four children as the story's protagonists, is clearly heavily influenced by Stephen King's *It*."

Sorry, but I couldn't help but laugh when I read that. Sure, King has always been an influential author in my eyes, along with Poe, Bradbury, McCammon, and Lansdale. But, despite their assumptions, *Hell Hollow* was *not* influenced by *It*. In fact, quite honestly, *It* has never been in my top ten list of favorite King books

(I found the whole "cosmic turtle" sub-plot to be confusing and the sex-sharing scene between Beverly and the boys in Pennywise's catacombs to be unnecessary and a bit embarrassing). It was probably the furthest book from my mind when I was writing about the children of Harmony's encounter – and subsequent battle – with the reincarnated evil of Doctor Augustus Leech, a magic-wielding bounty hunter of souls for Satan and his otherworldly kingdom.

This comparison would have never been made back in 1996, when the book was originally scheduled to see publication. That's because the classic "coming-of-age" novel was alive and well back then. Almost every author in the genre in the horror hey-day of the 80s and 90s had done at least one. My favorites during that period were King's "The Body" (brought to film as "Stand By Me), Robert R. McCammon's *Boy's Life*, - Dan Simmon's *Summer of Night*, and Ray Bradbury's - *Something Wicked this Way Comes*. Even before then, I had my mainstream favorites; *To Kill a Mockingbird, Catcher in the Rye, and The Lord of the Flies.*

For those of you out there who are a little hazy about exactly what a "coming-of-age" story is, it is a tale of one (or several) youths taking a bold step toward adulthood due to adventurous or devastating circumstances, as well as a loss of innocence or naivety in the face of conflict or seemingly unsurmountable odds of survival. Once, a horror author naturally gravitated toward the writing of such a novel, simply to explore their own childhood trials and tribulations and, in some cases, to exorcise demons from years past. I, myself, had written two other coming-of-age novels before *Hell Hollow*. One had been my first novel, *Hindsight*, in which Cindy Ann Biggs, a nine-year-old girl during the Great Depression uses her gift of second sight (gained after a long bout of Typhoid Fever) to solve a brutal triple-murder that had taken place in an abandoned tobacco barn and, in turn, protect herself and her family from the wrath of the perpetrators. The second one was *Fear*, which most fans believe my best work to date. In *Fear*, a young farm boy named Jeb Sweeny discovers that a ravenous snake-critter is on the rampage in his community, slaughtering livestock and abducting small children. His only chance in conquering it is to journey to the neighboring providence of Fear County, a place full of evil and deadly dangers... a place where every childhood nightmare exists as dark reality.

As a reader, I love a good coming-of-age novel. I enjoy reading about children facing a greater, adult evil and eventually conquering it. It wasn't until I returned to the horror genre in 2006, that I discovered that coming-of-age novels weren't as popular as they had been during the first leg of my writing career in the late 80s to mid-90s. In fact, it seemed that my peers had stopped writing them completely. Oh, I was fortunate enough to find a few gems here and there; Joe Lansdale's *The Bottoms*, James Newman's *Midnight Rain*, and much of John R. Little's excellent altered-time fiction, including *The Memory Tree*, *Miranda*, and his upcoming offering, *Secrets*. But for the most part, today's horror writer seems to prefer to deal solely with adult situations and characters. Many believe the use of children as protagonists is passe'. I don't happen to be one of those who hold that opinion, which puts me in the minority these days. More than anything else, that was why *Hell Hollow* was so unfairly compared to - *It*; today's new breed of horror reader/critic/reviewer didn't grow up in the Golden Age of horror fiction and, so, does not hold the same appreciation for the coming-of-age story as some of my past contemporaries and I do. It is probably also the reason why *HH* - was viewed as a "throwback to the days of 90's pulp paperback horror", which essentially it is, since it was written during that time and contains that same flavor of fun, adventure, and fantastical horror.

Will the coming-of-age novel enjoy a resurgence... or will its popularity wane to the point of no return and readers will have nothing but adult-based fiction to enjoy? I very much doubt that the latter will occur. The coming-of-age story has been popular for centuries, from the Bible (the tales of Joseph and his coat of many colors and David and Goliath) to young adult classics like *Little Women, Anne of Green Gables, The Yearling,* and *Treasure Island.* Childhood and its joys and triumphs, as well as its trials and tragedies, should be a part of one's intellectual and emotional make-up; a part to be cherished and revisited from time to time. It shouldn't be set on a shelf to gather dust, buried in the back yard, or traded in for the no-nonsense life of an adult, never to be enjoyed or remembered again. That is the great thing about the coming-of-age novel; it returns you to a time when you didn't have to worry about bills, failing health, war, or income taxes. It was a time when a 64-count box of Crayolas opened a world of creativity, Santa Claus and the Easter Bunny were as flesh-and-blood real as your mother and father, and playing cowboys and Indians, or cops and robbers transported you to a realm of the imagination that was a child's equivalent of living those lives through novels and motion pictures.

If we are lucky, it won't be long until a new generation of writers look past the hard-core aspects of horror fiction and decide that the coming-of-age novel is, indeed, a viable and worthwhile addition to their collective body of literary works. As for me, I'll certainly do my part to keep that particular sub-genre of child-versus-evil fiction alive and kicking.

Way Down South in the Dark of Dixie: Writing Southern Horror Fiction

W hat is it about the American South that makes you uneasy and creeps you out? Is the terrain? The dark woods and lonesome hollows? The Appalachian Mountains shrouded with mist or the Spanish moss laced bayous of Louisiana? Maybe it's the isolated stretch of rural highway with no streetlights to speak of or the abandoned farmhouse down the road, that in your mind, is most certainly haunted? It could be the people. Not the good, decent folks that practice Southern hospitality, but the other kind. The ones you saw in movies like *Deliverance*, *Southern Comfort*, or *The Texas Chainsaw Massacre*. Maybe it is some of the more sordid and unforgivable events of Southern history that bother you; slavery, the Klan, racial injustice, or Martin Luther King falling to a gunshot on the second-floor balcony of the Lorraine Motel in Memphis.

Yes, there certainly seem to be plenty of things to unsettle and potentially frighten you about the states south of the Mason-Dixon Line. I reckon that is why I've spent thirty-five years of my writing career spinning tales of Southern-fried horror. For some of you it's a place of potential danger and disaster. For me, well, it's simply... home.

The sub-genre of Southern horror is a specialized one and there are only a few of us in dark fiction who devote ourselves to it wholeheartedly. Those authors who write the stuff and do it damn good include Robert McCammon, Joe R. Lansdale, Elizabeth Massie, James Newman, and John Quick, as well as storytellers of past generations like Manly Wade Wellman, Michael McDowell, and Karl Edward Wagner. In his 1991 anthology *Borderlands 3*, Thomas F. Monteleone had this to say about it: *"There is a sub-genre that seems to have come to life on its own – a kind of spontaneous generation once ascribed to maggots on dead meat or that coiling swirl of dust balls in the corner of an abandoned house. It's called Southern Horror, and it's marked largely by a preying upon the natural urban paranoia of the rest of us, i.e. those of us who don't live in places called "vales" or "corners" or "hollows". It is marked by a strong regional flavor, a familiarity with custom and superstition, and a style that can't be faked."*

So, you might ask, what region constitutes the territory of Southern Horror?

Generally, the states considered to make up "The South" are Alabama, Arkansas, Florida, Georgia, Louisiana, Mississippi, North Carolina, South Carolina,

Tennessee, Texas, and Virginia. I tend to include Kentucky and West Virginia because, in my opinion, they are just as Southern in custom and tradition as the others are. After all, any place that features a life-sized statue of the Mothman prominently on its town square has to be Southern in nature... and, if it isn't, it certainly ought to be.

The two main ingredients that make Southern horror work best are characterization and setting. If you have engaging, flesh-and-blood characters and credible locales that readers can step comfortably (or, better yet, uncomfortably) into and walk around, the writer has won half the battle. Add a dark and credible plot to the mix – one that the reader feels that they are personally involved and invested in – and the short story or novel is on its way to being solid and memorable.

There has always been a moral chasm between light and darkness in Southern culture; one that is as divisive as a line drawn in the sand, or as we like to say, " being on the right or wrong side of the tracks". On one side lies the get-up-and-get-ready-for-church crowd; those who relish normalcy and embrace family heritage... the kind who enjoy sitting on their front porches on a warm, sunny afternoon, spinning tall tales and indulging in a cold glass of sweet tea and a slice of Mama's pecan pie. On the other, lies the wild bunch; midnight drag racers and hellacious honky-tonk patrons. Drinkers of rotgut whiskey and home-brewed moonshine, barroom brawlers, and backwoods "yokels" with an unhealthy fascination for honed steel and firearms.

Traditionally in Southern horror, the former group is the protagonists and the latter the antagonists, although lately there has been more of a gray area surfacing between the two... a blurring of that long-standing line. Often in current fiction, the religious right, particularly the more fanatical factions, are depicted as the evil threat, while those once considered to be "heathens" and "no-account rednecks" have become the acceptable "everyman" protagonist, in a gritty, anti-hero sort of way. Personally, I tend to be old school in my characterizations, relying on past folks that I've known or known of, to build my cast of characters. I do, however, shuffle the deck sometimes and go against the grain. There is nothing more satisfying than to have the small town outcast – the one that folks despise and consider to be utterly useless to society – come out of nowhere and save the day.

In my own writing, I have discovered that coming-of-age tales meld very well with the dynamics of Southern horror. Jeb Sweeny in *Fear*, Cindy Ann in *Hindsight*, and Keith and the gang in *Hell Hollow*... all are ordinary kids battling the worse kinds of rural evil, be it a slithering snake-critter from a hellish county, a transient mass murderer in a pickup truck, or the spirit of a soul-stealing traveling medicine show man inhabiting the body of a serial killer. One of my all-time favorite coming-of-age novels set in the South is Robert McCammon's *Boy's Life*, which depicts rural life in Alabama with incredible heart and versatility. The wasp attack during the church service is truly a classic. Another is Joe Lansdale's *The Bottoms*, a Depression-era murder mystery set in a small Texas town, in which a young boy and his sister discover the body of a black woman in the bottoms of the Sabine River, brutally murdered by an apparent serial killer. It is tense, atmospheric, and thought provoking, and, along with *Boy's Life*, one of my favorite coming-of-age novels of the Deep South.

Setting also has a great deal to do with the mood and believability of tales of outhern horror. Lonesome backroads, particularly those winding through dense forest or stretching across acre upon acre of deserted pastureland, can practically lead to anywhere and spawn terror and dread for the reader. After all, in such places of isolation, there is no one around to hear you scream. In turn, the hills and hollows, peaks and valleys, of the Appalachian Mountains are steeped heavily in superstition and dark folklore. The legends and mythos of Appalachia, from Virginia clear down to Georgia, serve as useful fodder for the Southern-fried story mill. In fact, Appalachia is known to have more sightings of mysterious cryptids than anywhere else in the United States. These include all manner of legendary mountain monsters such as the Tennessee Wildman, Ol' Orange Eyes, Phantom Cats, Sheepquatch, Devil Monkeys, the Wampus Beast, and the Grassman, just to name a few.

One location that's rarely explored in Southern storytelling, but can be used to great effect, is the fetid swamps and dark bayous of Louisiana. That region is one of my personal favorites to explore. I have penned several Cajun and Creole horror tales over the years, including *The Web of La Sanguinaire, Beneath Black Bayou, Mojo Mama,* and *Suckers!* I particularly love to write Cajun dialogue. The rhythm of speech is quirky, unique, and fun to depict on the written page. Also, there are numerous creepy-crawlers and swamp critters to make bayou stories entertaining and cringe-inducing; creatures such as alligators, snakes, spiders, lizards, gars, and leeches... all sufficiently dreadful and icky in nature.

Texas is a state that most folks don't immediately consider to be Southern, but actually is. Joe Lansdale has written much about the more temperate and wooded area of East Texas, but West Texas should also be included in the Southern horror canon. I've explored the Lone Star State many times, in such short stories as "Dust Devils", "Thinning the Herd", and "Flesh-Welder", and in my second Zebra novel, *Pitfall*, in which a brood of hungry Tasmanian devils invade a sleepy, West Texas town.

Like many regional writers, those who specialize in Southern horror tend to focus the lion's share of their work on territory that is intimately familiar to them. Although I have written stories that encompass all the states of Dixie, most of them take place in my home state of Tennessee. Basing your fiction in a community or small town similar to the one you grew up in, or amid a dark and isolated stretch of woods that you once played in as a child, give your story a tone of authenticity that is difficult to accomplish if you are writing about a place you have never actually seen or experienced before. Furthermore, physical senses can kick in, triggering a mutual connection in the mind of the reader. The smell of wood smoke in the air or the dry, musky odor of an old house that has sat unoccupied for far too long. Or maybe the roar of a distant freight train and the mournful wailing of its whistle, or the lonesome call of a whippoorwill , the chirring of crickets in dewy grass, and the monotonous peeping of toads along a backwoods creek bed.

Inspiration for rural horror tales can come from numerous sources. Regional legends and ghost stories, family and local history, mysterious happenings and unsolved crimes can all spark engaging storylines. Many of my early short stories and novels were inspired by tales told to me by my grandmother and mother. Stories of local hauntings and true folks you'd not want to run into in the dead of night, as well as ancestors who had fought in the Civil War, both for the Blue and the Gray, including others who had headed out west, either to seek fortune ahead of them or flee from trouble dogging their heels from behind. In fact, I absorbed so many family stories that took place during the Great Depression or during and after World War II, that I discovered that I could write effectively in those time periods with very little or no research whatsoever. I mostly attribute that skill to my grandmother and her engaging way with spinning a tale. A good storyteller – be it vocally or through prose – can impart an infectious sense of time and place that transcends the mind and sinks directly into the soul.

In the world of horror fiction, regionalism gives the reader an opportunity to break the bounds of their mundane life and take a journey beyond the confines of the armchair, however distressing and frightening it might be, into a realm beyond their own. Tales of Southern horror have much to offer in the way of chills and nightmarish tableaus, as well as a welcome reprieve from various horror locations and tropes that have been greatly overused in the past.

Inventory of Fears : Fuel for the Horror-Writing Mind

For the past couple of months, I've been working on a project with Cemetery Dance Publications; writing personalized horror stories for folks who want to see themselves as the main character. This involves taking them, their families, and their everyday lives, and pretty much placing them within the worse nightmare imaginable... implementing their own fears and phobias. This has been a challenging project to say the least, since I have always had to depend on my own personal list of fears and horrors to use as fodder for my tales of Southern horror. Going beyond my comfort zone -- writing-wise -- and using the terrors of actual living and breathing people (versus purely fictional characters) has been an eye-opening exercise, but one I wouldn't have missed for the world.

Lately, I've been thinking about my own fears and phobias. Sometimes they bob to the surface -- like a bloated body from the bottom of a deep lake -- within my fiction. Other times they remain buried, waiting patiently for their turn on the page. Today I sat down and jotted down a list of my worst fears, just to see how many I had. As it turned out, I ended up having more than I first thought. Here they are, in no particular order....

1. Fear of Snakes: This is a common enough fear; alot of folks suffer from it. But I loathe the things. It doesn't matter if they're poisonous or harmless, alive or dead... they completely freak me out. Part of my snake phobia originates from some of my Grandmama Spicer's snake tales, told to me at an early age. Tales of eighteen foot rattlers that reared up out of the mud of a logging road like a cobra, of multi-colored serpents slithering along the rafters overhead before dropping upon unsuspecting sleepers, and that goosebump-raising tale about the girl who drank from a stream and ending up housing a snake within her body into adulthood (which Grandmama claimed to be a true medical case). I later turned that tall-tale into story called "Miss Abigail's Delicate Condition". My grandfather, Pappy Spicer, seemed to be constantly vexed by snakes during his long life, having been bitten several times by copperheads. One time he was taking his morning constitutional in the outhouse when a chicken snake fell off the rafters and landed slap-dab in his lap. That's enough to scare the crap out of anyone!

2. Fear of Heights: I've always had an extremely bad case of vertigo. I can't go three steps up a ladder without getting the shakes. And I have trouble looking over the edge of a cliff or bluff, even if there's a fence or barrier there to prevent me from plunging to my death. I attribute this phobia to an incident that happened in the 5th grade. Me and another classmate had climbed to the very top of the jungle gym, when the school bully prevented us from climbing down, chucking rocks at us, nearly causing us to fall several times, until the recess bell rang. Since that day, I can't stand to be away from solid ground, especially if my footing isn't 100% rock steady.

3. Fear of Burns: I am mortified of being burned. Whenever my children get too close to a stove eye, a clothes iron, or a pot of boiling water, I nearly get hysterical. This phobia also has its roots in my past. When I was two and half, I was visiting my aunt's house. I was playing, while my aunt and mother sat in the kitchen and drank coffee. On the stove sat one of those big ol' silver coffee percolators. Carelessly, the electrical cord was stretched across the kitchen doorway and plugged into an outlet on the opposite wall. I was dancing around and singing a song about a choo-choo train and, when it came to the part about blowing the whistle, I reckon I just had to grab something and give it a yank. And you guessed it... the thing I yanked was that power cord. That percolator -- full of hot coffee -- came crashing down on top of me. It missed my head by inches, but scalded my left arm. I don't know what degree burn it was, but it required skin grafts to repair the damage. That horrifying episode fortified my fear of hot things (although my scarred arm did help teach me the difference between right and left at an early age.) It also played a big part in my writing of "Dead Skin".

4. Fear of Spiders: I've always had a phobia of spiders. Like snakes, they don't have to be poisonous either. If they have eight legs, that's a good enough reason to avoid them. Down here in Tennessee, brown recluse spiders are common (or fiddlebacks, as we call them) and there's even a jumping spider that lurks in the woods that will literally chase after you if you don't put some spark in your step. I remember when I was little, me and my brother, Kevin, would play in the garage next to a wall that was half concrete block and half drywall. In between the two sections was a thick strip of tar paper. We liked to play in a particular spot and played there all summer long. Later on, my father tore the tar paper loose and, underneath, was a nest of black widow spiders. They had been lurking there all along, directly over our heads! My spider stories include "The Web of La Sanguinaire" and "Housewarming". (By the way, take a look at that hungry little gal below. Doesn't that give you the creeps just looking at it?)

5. Fear of unfamiliar places: I've always had a bad feeling about places I've never been before, especially while traveling. Whenever we get off an interstate exit, there's a sense of potential danger at being at a place in time where there's no one but complete strangers around. It's not so bad at exits where there are a dozen fast food joints and hotels, but at the exits where there might be a single gas station or a country store (if you're lucky) the atmosphere seems downright threatening. I remember when I was about seven, we took a road trip. We didn't take the interstate back then, but traveled the rural highways to take us from point A to point B. My father stopped at this little country Texaco station and was short-changed by the station attendant. When he went back inside to confront the man -- a lanky, grease monkey of a redneck -- the mechanic started cussing and bullying him. I mean this fella was downright mean, yelling and waving his arms. I remember cowering in the back seat, thinking "He could kill Daddy! He could kill us all and repaint our car and sell it and nobody would ever know what happened to us!" I still think about that unnerving pitstop when I'm traveling with my family. My story "Exit 85" sort of sums up my fears of stopping at places where folks don't want you around... or do, for all the wrong reasons.

6. Fear of Clowns: My fear of clowns isn't as intense as it once was. I guess that's something that has diminished with age. When I was a kid, though, about the only clown who didn't make me want to pee my pants was Bozo. Since the horror genre has capitalized quite a bit on the evil or killer clown, it's apparent that a whole lot of people possess this phobia. Clowns are just plain creepy. Don't forget, Pennywise was a clown. So was John Wayne Gacy. And remember Jimmy Stewart in The Greatest Show on Earth? The movie where he played a fugitive in floppy shoes, who never takes his makeup off, even between shows? That's what freaks me out. Anyone could be hiding behind the grease paint and red rubber nose. It could be a good, decent guy... or it could be a child molesting cannibal. How could you ever tell... until it was too late?

7. Fear of folks who are missing part of their body: Yeah, I know... awful ain't it? I mean, I have nothing against people who were unfortunate enough to lose an arm or a leg or other appendage for one reason or another, but I still have this irrational fear of being around them. Maybe it's just the awkwardness of being in their presence and wondering what happened to them. You just can't go up to them and flat-out ask them what happened to their missing part. Oh, there are some who will tell you way more than you want to know... about how they slipped and fell into a buzzsaw and sliced off their arm, clean as a whistle. Others don't want to discuss it at all... perhaps for a good reason. I've worked in enough factories during my lifetime to come across three or four folks with missing hands or fingers. One thing about machines... right when you think they'll do one thing, they'll call you a bald-faced liar and do just the opposite. And sometimes that involves maiming and mangling. One of the fears of a woman I just wrote a story for was a fear of prosthetic devices. She was a nurse and one night in the ER she came across a patient with a prosthetic face. He had lost most of his real face to a flesh-eating fungus and was forced to wear a fake face to cover it up. When I read this on her questionnaire, the image of the man with the prosthetic face took command and totally motivated the plot... which turned out to be one of the creepiest stories I've ever written, in my opinion.

So, for a horror writer, I reckon a good long list of fears and phobias might be a big plus. I know I put mine to good use. Of course, my list lengthens every now and then... especially when I watch the evening news. I'm always amazed -- and mortified -- at the amount of cruelty and evil some folks can dish out to their fellow man, and they can be mighty creative at it. As long as they shock society with their sick shenanigans, we writers of dark fiction will never be at a loss of something horrifying to write about.

Acknowledgments

I would like to thank the following folks for the love, friendship, and support that they have provided over the years. Some were there at the best of times, some at the very worst. All are greatly loved and appreciated .

Joyce Kelly, Reilly, Makenna, and Ryan Kelly, Kevin and Theresa Kelly, Katie and Jared Clement, Karen Kelly, Chase Reeves, Richard Chizmar, Joe R. Lansdale, James Newman, Brian Keene, Mary SanGiovanni, Hunter Goatley, Tod Clark, Stephen Shrewsbury, Bryan Smith, Joshua Bilmes, Mark Rainey, Elizabeth Massie, David Niall Wilson, David Dobbs, Mark & Carletta Hickerson, Steven Barnes, Alex McVey, Zach McCain, Keith Minnion, Alan M. Clark, Justin T. Coons, Tom Monteleone, Paul Goblirsch, Leigh Haig, Ken McKinley, Kenneth Cain, Jarod Barbee, Jeremy Wagner, Patrick C. Harrison III, Roy Robbins, Michelle Garza, Melissa Lason, Chris Lason, Mark Sieber, Patrick McDonough, Brennan LaFaro, J. Rodney Turner, Nicholas Gray, Dawn Shea, Kevin Lucia, John R. Little, Adam James, Brad Saenz, Robert Brouhard, Ruthann Jagge, Deb Soward Yudenfriend, Bridgett Nelson, R.E. Sargent, Jason Brannon, Ed Myers,

Randy Myers, Stephen Groves, Rodney Canavan, Tosha Gulley, Glenn Davis, John Boden, Theresa Bowen, Daniel Volpe, Jenny Penuel, Christian Götz, Ginny Skipper, Jeremy Harden, Mike Rankin, Sonora Bostian-Posner, Todd Keisling, Tim Meyer, Glen Rolfe, Samuel Smith, Robert Essig, Tara Losacano, Robb Carter, Heather Collins, Patti Switzer Tindal, Alice Diech, Bob McCredie, Marina Schnierer, Victoria, Smith, Paul Little, Edward Sizemore, H Michael Casper, Chuck Knight, Alan Saul, Gwen Sergent, Tyler Cooper, Jeanne and Brian Coleman, Keith Adam Luethke, Lance Dale, Scott Magill, Donald Belcher, Jeff Strand, Lynne Hansen, Glenn Rolfe, Wesley Southard, Jonathan Janz, Hunter Shea, Mercedes Yardley, Steve Stred, Duncan Ralston, Ronald Malfi, Ty Schwamberger, Steve Vernon, Kristopher Triana, Kevin J. Kennedy, D. Christopher Tatum, Chad Lutzke, John Durgin, Jeremy Helper, Sidney Williams, Glenn Rolfe, Adam Cesare, Tim Waggoner, Michael Knost, Eugene Johnson, Fran Friel, Cina Pelayo, Kelli Owen, Bob Ford, Vivian R. Kasley, John Quick, Nikki Noir, Janine Pipe, Kenzie, Jennings, Laurel Hightower, Hailey Piper, Eric LaRocca, Gabino Iglesias, Samantha Kolesnik, Tyler Jones, John Palisano, Michael Clark, Chris Miller, Carver Pike, Fred Nocito, Randy Chandler, Beth Williams, Mary Danner, Stephen Knowles, Mort Castle, Randy Fox, Troy Guinn, Lowell Cunningham, Lindsey Cunningham, Gary Raisor, Kevin Whitten, Brad Proctor, Jason Grell, Alex Brown, Andrew Fowlow, Cameron Chaney, Sadie Hartmann, Michelle Reed, Erica Robyn Metcalf, S.D.Vassallo, Kelly LeBeouf, Melissa Sinicki.

About the Author

RONALD KELLY was born November 20, 1959, in Nashville, Tennessee. He attended Pegram Elementary School and Cheatham County Central High School, and, during his junior and senior years, had aspirations of become a comic book artist before his interests turned to writing fiction.

Ronald Kelly began his professional writing career in the horror genre in 1986 with the sale of his first short story, "Breakfast Serial" to *Terror Time Again* magazine. Specializing in tales of Southern horror, his work was widely published in magazines such as *Deathrealm, Grue, New Blood, Eldritch Tales,* and *Cemetery Dance.* His first novel, *Hindsight,* was released by Zebra Books in 1990. He wrote for Zebra for six years, publishing such novels as *Pitfall, Something Out There, Father's*

Little Helper, The Possession, Fear, Blood Kin, and *Moon of the Werewolf (Undertaker's Moon).* His audiobook collection, *Dark Dixie: Tales of Southern Horror,* was included on the nominating ballot of the 1992 Grammy Awards for Best Spoken Word or Non-Musical Album. Ronald's short fiction work has been published in major anthologies such as *Cold Blood, Borderlands 3, Dark at Heart, Shock Rock, Hot Blood: Seeds of Fear, The Earth Strikes Back,* and many more,

In the mid-1990s, the bottom dropped out of the mass-market horror market. When Zebra canceled their horror line in October 1996, Ronald Kelly stopped writing for ten years and worked various jobs including welder, factory worker, production manager, drugstore manager, and custodian. In 2006, Kelly returned to the horror genre and began writing again. In early 2008, Croatoan Publishing released his work Flesh Welder as a stand-alone chapbook, and it quickly sold out. In early 2009 Cemetery Dance Publications released a hardcover edition of his first short story collection, *Midnight Grinding & Other Twilight Terrors.* Also in 2010, Cemetery Dance released his first novel in over ten years, *Hell Hollow,* as a hardcover edition. Between 2011 and 2015, Kelly's Zebra horror novels were released in limited hardcover editions by Thunderstorm Books as *The Essential Ronald Kelly series.* Each book contained a new novella related to the novel's original storyline.

After his comeback to the horror genre, he has written several additional novels, such as *Restless Shadows, Timber Gray,* and *The Buzzard Zone,* as well as numerous short story collections: *After the Burn, Mister Glow-Bones & Other Halloween Tales, The Halloween Store & Other Tales of All-Hallows' Eve, Season's Creepings: Tales of Holiday Horror, Irish Gothic,* and *The Web of La Sanguinaire & Other Arachnid Horrors.* In 2021, his collection of extreme horror stories, *The Essential Sick Stuff,* published by Silver Shamrock Publications, won the Splatterpunk Award for Best Collection. He is currently publishing two new horror series: *The Saga of Dead-Eye* and the EC Comics-inspired *Southern-Fried* story collections with Crossroad Press.

Ronald Kelly lives in a backwoods hollow in Brush Creek, Tennessee, sixty miles east of Nashville, with his wife and young'uns.

Bibliography

The Last Halloween, was originally published in
October Dreams 2: A Celebration of Halloween by
Cemetery Dance First Edition January 2016

**SADDLES, SIX-SHOOTERS, & SEX : Writing for
the Jake Logan Series**, was originally published in
the blog, Southern-Fried & Horrified: News & Notions
From Horror Author Ronald Kelly / March 2019.

**Prose Mechanics Evolution! : How the Writing
Process has Changed Over the Past 45 Years**, was
originally published as a guest post for Nightworms Blog,
January 2021.

**Walking the Fence Rail : Balancing Faith and
Horror Writing**, was originally published in the blog
Southern-Fried & Horrified: News & Notions From
Horror Author Ronald Kelly / August 2013.

**A Word from the Pulp-Writing, Zebra-Striped,
Retro-90s Horror Hack**, was originally published in
the blog Southern-Fried & Horrified: News & Notions
From Horror Author Ronald Kelly / August 2013.

<u>Where Are the Children? : The Decline of the Coming-of-Age Novel</u>, was originally published in the blog, Southern-Fried & Horrified: News & Notions From Horror Author Ronald Kelly / September 2013.

<u>Way Down South in the Dark of Dixie : Writing Southern Horror Fiction</u>, was originally published in *Writers Workshop of Horror 2* by Hydra Publications September 2021.

<u>Inventory of Fears : Fuel for the Horror-Writing Mind</u>, was originally published in the blog, Southern-Fried & Horrified: News & Notions From Horror Author Ronald Kelly / March 2010.

Also By Ronald Kelly

Novels

Hindsight (1990)
Pitfall (1990)
Something Out There / The Dark'Un (1991)
Moon of the Werewolf / Undertaker's Moon (1991)
Father's Little Helper / Twelve Gauge (1992)
The Possession / Burnt Magnolia (1993)
Fear (1994)
Blood Kin (1996)
Hell Hollow (2010)
Timber Gray (2010)
The China Doll (2011)
Restless Shadows (2014)
The Buzzard Zone (2018)

Collections
Dark Dixie: Tales of Southern Horror (1991)
Midnight Grinding & Other Twilight Terrors (2009)
The Sick Stuff (2010)
Twilight Hankerings (2010)
Unhinged (2011)

Cumberland Furnace & Other Fear-Forged Fables (2011)
After the Burn (2011)
Long Chills (2013)
Mister Glow-Bones & Other Halloween Tales (2014)
Midnight Tide & Other Seaside Shivers (2016)
More Sick Stuff (2019)
The Essential Sick Stuff (2020)
The Halloween Store & Other Tales of All Hallows' Eve (2020)
Season's Creepings: Tales of Holiday Horror (2020)
Irish Gothic: Tales of Celtic Horror (2021)
The Web of La Sanguinaire & Other Arachnid Horrors (2021)

Chapbooks
Flesh Welder (2007)
Tanglewood (2008)
Strong Steps (2016)

Series

The Saga of Dead-Eye
Book One: Vampires, Zombies, & Mojo Men (2021)
Book Two: Werewolves, Swamp Creatures, & Hellacious Haints (2022)

Southern-Fried EC Horror Collection
Book One: Haunt of Southern-Fried Fear (2022)
Book Two: Tales from the Southern-Fried Crypt (to be announced)